CONTENTS

An Introduction from Alli 4

How *Spirit-Led Bible Study* Works 6

Who Is the Holy Spirit? 8

Session 1 • Observation 12

How-To Practice: Observation 22

Session 2 • Listening 40

How-To Practice: Listening 54

Session 3 • Orientation 70

How-To Practice: Orientation 82

Session 4 • Prayer 108

How-To Practice: Prayer 120

Session 5 • Context 132

How-To Practice: Context 144

Session 6 • Action 156

How-To Practice: Action 170

About the Author 187

Appendix A 188

Appendix B 189

Appendix C 192

AN INTRODUCTION FROM ALLI

I wrote *Spirit-Led Bible Study* to help you discover fresh ways of engaging Scripture and a deeper connection to the Word of God. In this study, you will explore passages from the Bible and follow the Holy Spirit to new places of understanding, discovery, and truth. The Bible has so many layers, and God knows exactly where to take you to find life through His Word.

This study has six sessions that will introduce you to six Bible-study practices. Each practice is designed for you to seek personal interaction with the Spirit combined with a foundational principle of Bible study. It's only through faith in Jesus that the Spirit lives within you, so the starting point for this study is *receiving Jesus Christ as your Lord and Savior.* You have to begin with His Spirit of Truth inside you since we are counting on Him to lead!

I hope you end this study more alive and in love with the written and living Word of God. The best outcome of these six sessions would be a deeper connection to Jesus through your Bible. However, no amount of Bible-study rigor will ever, in and of itself, produce a life in God. Jesus said to the Jewish leaders, "You study the Scriptures diligently because you think that in them you have eternal life. These are the very Scriptures that testify about me, yet you refuse to come to me to have life" (John 5:39–40). This word is still true, so in *Spirit-Led Bible Stud*y we will practice coming to Jesus with an eager, open heart in His Word. ***Life** in Christ* is the best goal of Bible study—not just knowledge of Scripture.

However, reading and studying Scripture requires some diligence and skill. Good Bible-study principles and practices are necessary to uncover actual meaning and get to know who God really is. His true character, heart, and mercy toward us in Christ become clearer with good study practices. So, I want to help you study well to find all His love and life within the Word.

This study will meet you where you are, whether this is your first Bible study or you've been doing them for years. All you need is this study guide and your

SIX SESSIONS WITH VIDEO ACCESS

SPIRIT-LED BIBLE STUDY

SIX PRACTICES TO BRING THE BIBLE TO LIFE

Alli Patterson

HarperChristian Resources

Spirit-Led Bible Study
Copyright © 2026 by Alli Patterson

Published by HarperChristian Resources, 3950 Sparks Drive SE, Suite 101, Grand Rapids, MI 49546, USA.
HarperChristian Resources is a registered trademark of HarperCollins Christian Publishing, Inc.

Requests for information should be addressed to customercare@harpercollins.com.

ISBN 978-0-310-17613-8 (softcover)
ISBN 978-0-310-17614-5 (ebook)

Unless otherwise noted, Scripture quotations are taken from the Holy Bible, New International Version®, NIV®. Copyright © 1973, 1978, 1984, 2011 by Biblica, Inc.® Used by permission. All rights reserved worldwide. The "NIV" and "New International Version" are trademarks registered in the United States Patent and Trademark Office by Biblica, Inc.®

Scripture quotations marked AMPC are taken from the Amplified® Bible (AMPC). Copyright © 1954, 1958, 1962, 1964, 1965, 1987 by The Lockman Foundation. Used by permission. www.lockman.org.

Scripture quotations marked CSB are taken from the Christian Standard Bible®. Copyright © 2017 by Holman Bible Publishers. Used by permission. Christian Standard Bible® and CSB® are federally registered trademarks of Holman Bible Publishers.

Scripture quotations marked MSG are taken from The Message. Copyright © 1993, 2002, 2018 by Eugene H. Peterson. Used by permission of NavPress. All rights reserved. Represented by Tyndale House Publishers, Inc.

Scripture quotations marked NASB are taken from the (NASB®) New American Standard Bible®. Copyright © 1960, 1971, 1977, 1995, 2020 by The Lockman Foundation. Used by permission. All rights reserved. www.lockman.org.

Scripture quotations marked NIrV are taken from the Holy Bible, New International Reader's Version®, NIrV®. Copyright © 1995, 1996, 1998, 2014 by Biblica, Inc.® Used by permission of Zondervan. All rights reserved worldwide. www.zondervan.com. The "NIrV" and "New International Reader's Version" are trademarks registered in the United States Patent and Trademark Office by Biblica, Inc.®

Scripture quotations marked NKJV are taken from the New King James Version®. Copyright © 1982 by Thomas Nelson. Used by permission. All rights reserved.

Scripture quotations marked NLT are taken from the Holy Bible, New Living Translation. Copyright © 1996, 2004, 2015 by Tyndale House Foundation. Used by permission of Tyndale House Publishers, Carol Stream, Illinois 60188. All rights reserved.

Any internet addresses (websites, blogs, etc.) and telephone numbers in this study guide are offered as a resource. They are not intended in any way to be or imply an endorsement by HarperChristian Resources, nor does HarperChristian Resources vouch for the content of these sites and numbers for the life of this study guide.

All rights reserved. No portion of this book may be reproduced, stored in a retrieval system, or transmitted in any form or by any means—electronic, mechanical, photocopy, recording, scanning, or other—except for brief quotations in critical reviews or articles, without the prior written permission of the publisher.

HarperChristian Resources titles may be purchased in bulk for church, business, fundraising, or ministry use. For information, please email ResourceSpecialist@ChurchSource.com.

The author is represented by Alive Literary Agency, www.aliveliterary.com.

Without limiting the exclusive rights of any author, contributor or the publisher of this publication, any unauthorized use of this publication to train generative artificial intelligence (AI) technologies is expressly prohibited. HarperCollins also exercise their rights under Article 4(3) of the Digital Single Market Directive 2019/790 and expressly reserve this publication from the text and data mining exception.

HarperCollins Publishers, Macken House, 39/40 Mayor Street Upper, Dublin 1, D01 C9W8, Ireland (https://www.harpercollins.com).

Art direction: Ron Huizinga
Cover Design: Michelle Lenger
Interior Design: Lauren Rives

First Printing November 2025 / Printed in the United States of America

Bible to complete each session, but you may run across instances where you want to investigate something with external resources. You can learn surprisingly deep things in maps, genealogies, and timelines! This endeavor may require tools and practice in understanding the cultures, languages, and historical eras in which the Scriptures were written. Rather than a classic Bible study with predetermined steps, this is a personal pursuit. That means I can't fully anticipate all the places you might want to go, but I have included some basic resources throughout the study that could be helpful. Though this study can be completed with only your Bible, it wouldn't surprise me if you went in search of more. Go for it! Just bring your learning back to your group so everyone will benefit.

As a student of the Bible, I care deeply about reading it well and pursuing the true meaning of the words. As a follower of Christ, I put my trust in the Holy Spirit to lead me in all ways, every day. I created this method of Bible study to honor both of those things. Begin now by asking God to reveal Himself to you through these practices. I am confident He will answer this prayer; knowing your Father is a privilege promised to you in Christ. Let's follow the Spirit there together.

Alli Patterson

HOW *SPIRIT-LED BIBLE STUDY* WORKS

Spirit-Led Bible Study is made for groups with the hope of new practices learned being used by individuals ongoing. Don't hesitate to put new Bible readers in groups with those who are very experienced in Bible study. It's amazing the different things each person will see as a result!

The study has two basic parts:

Group Meeting

- Introduce Practice of the Week
- Review of Individual Practice (Sessions 2–6)
- Warm-Up
- Word of Encouragement
- Watch Video
- During-Video Group Practice
- Group Discussion
- Prep for Individual Practice
- Closing Prayer

Individual Practice

After your Group Meeting, Individual Practice pages are provided for just that—practicing what you learn in each session. There are three practice Scripture passages for each session. Work on these on your own as homework before returning to your group for the next session. (Your next meeting will start with a review.) As you go through the exercises for Individual Practice, the Spirit may just lead you somewhere you never expected!

I RECOMMEND APPROXIMATELY 4–8 PEOPLE IN A GROUP.

THERE IS NOTHING TO READ OR PREPARE BEFORE THE FIRST TIME YOUR GROUP GETS TOGETHER.

TRY EACH PRACTICE THREE TIMES!

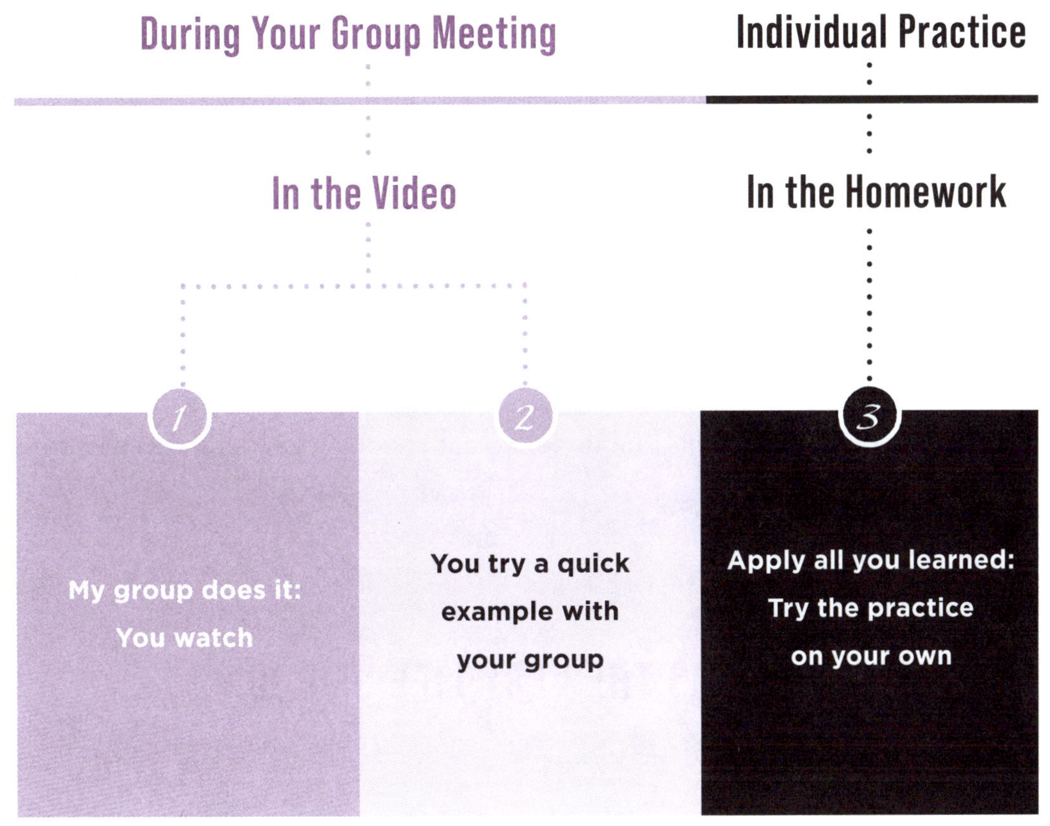

WHO IS THE HOLY SPIRIT?

The Holy Spirit is, as the Nicene Creed says, "the Lord, the giver of life." He is the very life of God. The Holy Spirit is very good news for all of us because we are born with a problem we cannot solve without Him. The problem is your heart: It is alienated from God even at birth and would never desire God on its own. There is no spark of divine life within you and, therefore, no hope of eternal life apart from God's intervention! He does that through His Spirit.

The Holy Spirit draws you toward Jesus before you know Him. When you receive Jesus as your Lord and Savior, the Spirit saves you by giving you a new heart (Ezekiel 36:26; John 3:3–8). It is only through the Spirit of God that you are reborn into a new life "in Christ" with a heart that truly desires God. The Holy Spirit then dwells in each and every believer. This is what Scripture calls baptism of the Spirit. This new life within you is not a "thing" you possess: God gives you *Himself!* Through the presence of the Spirit within you, you share in the eternal, beautiful life of the triune God who is Father, Son, and Holy Spirit.

As one of the three persons of the Holy Trinity, the Holy Spirit is fully God, equal but distinct from Father and Son (Mark 1:10–11). All three triune persons exist eternally (Isaiah 43:10), sharing one substance and equal in nature. All three are worthy of equal honor, obedience, and worship. Each of the three persons is distinct in consciousness (Acts 5:30–32) and personality, while sharing oneness of mind and will. The three are continuously connected in a warm, loving relationship.

HE IS THE VERY LIFE OF GOD.

The Holy Spirit is ever-present within believers, so your life in Christ will continue to expand—delivering you from darkness, increasing your obedience to His ways, and stoking desire within you to do the good works to which you are called. He challenges your old self and exposes the work of Satan in your life. His desire for you is to be conformed to the image of Jesus and to mature in your faith. The Spirit carries on the ministry of Jesus everywhere, in every way—leading, counseling, teaching, protecting, convicting, and empowering believers.

The Holy Spirit uses Scripture to do His work. In Scripture He opens eyes to see who the Lord truly is, giving you the mind of Christ. He is called "the Counselor" and "the Spirit of truth" by Jesus in John 14:17 and 26 (CSB). Again, Jesus called the Spirit those names in John 15:26 (CSB), finishing by saying the Spirit would "testify about me." The Holy Spirit enlightens you, draws you, and, according to Romans 5:5, "God's love has been poured out into our hearts through the Holy Spirit, who has been given to us." The Holy Spirit is how you experience the kindness and love of your heavenly Father every day.

The Holy Spirit takes what belongs only to Jesus and shares it with you! Because of His Spirit you are considered a "child of God" (John 1:13 NIrV) and coheir with Christ. He guarantees you will share in the inheritance waiting for you in heaven. The Holy Spirit seals you into the body of Christ and creates unity and making a family from believers in all nations, tribes, and tongues. He gives gifts to be used for the benefit of others and the glory of the Father. He empowers you to live your life as part of God's mission on earth.

As you do this study, you do it in the company of believers across the world and over many generations who share in the life of the triune God—Father, Son, and Holy Spirit—and seek to live more deeply in it each day.

FINAL ENCOURAGEMENT

My final encouragement is to do the study according to the design! Going through the pattern of engagement three times for each practice will result in the confidence and comfort you need to make it a regular part of how you engage Scripture.

Multiple exposures increase the likelihood you will make it your own! We will go through each new Bible study practice one at a time, but as you learn them, you can combine the practices over time in a variety of ways as you read. And I hope you will!

Get ready for a fresh, personal, life-giving experience with the Word of God.

SESSION 1

OBSERVATION

GROUP MEETING

Leader, read aloud to the group.

Welcome to *Spirit-Led Bible Study* Session 1!

This week all you need are your eyes and the Bible. You are going to learn to *OBSERVE*. OBSERVATION is an art. This practice is not just seeing: It is the art of *noticing*. You are going to go beyond reading the words to cultivate awareness of what is there and discuss *why* it is there. Anyone can participate because nothing is beneath your notice in God's Word!

OBSERVATION is a purposely slow process, so don't be in a hurry!

A good detective must be skilled in certain techniques, such as knowing where to look for clues and how to go about finding them.

Robert Traina, *Methodical Bible Study*

WARM-UP

Leader, read these instructions aloud to the group before the timer begins.

Let's warm up by playing detective with the people in our group. We are going to OBSERVE *one another* for two minutes! You may have already noticed things about each person as they joined in with the group today.

When prompted, write down a few OBSERVATIONS about others in the group.

RULES: Be insightful. Look carefully. Affirm. Reflect. Be personal and rich in detail. You can always see more than you think you can when you take the time to truly notice someone! Ask the Holy Spirit to reveal something to you as you look around at others.

Be careful to *note only what is right in front of your eyes*! This means no assumptions or guesses or interpretations. This is literal OBSERVATION. Just notice what is there to see.

SET A 2:00 TIMER. GO!

MY 2-MINUTE OBSERVATIONS

Take a few minutes to go around and share your OBSERVATIONS. Challenge OBSERVATIONS that are interpretations, conclusions, or go beyond what one's eyes could have seen.

WORD OF ENCOURAGEMENT FROM ALLI

Leader, read this aloud or select a volunteer to read to the group.

OBSERVATION is the practice that has made me most confident with the Bible! It has the power to take you from an insecure Bible reader to a strong contributor to any discussion or study of God's Word. I have grown as a student and teacher of Scripture due, fundamentally, to cultivating this art. The more you practice good OBSERVATION, the more confidently you will own the truths you find revealed in the Bible—because you'll know exactly where they come from.

Good OBSERVATIONS focus entirely on the words on the page. The text of Scripture is your only concern. Good OBSERVATIONS are basic. Good OBSERVATIONS do not assign meaning, pass judgments, go beyond what the text says, assume emotions, or rest on things you may have been taught in the past. OBSERVATIONS simply say what your eyes can plainly see right on the page.

NOW IT'S TIME TO TURN ON THE SESSION 1 VIDEO.

WATCH SESSION 1 VIDEO

Leader, stream the video or play the DVD.

OBSERVATION PRACTICE NOTES

Capture anything you want to remember about this practice as you watch the video. These notes will help you when you OBSERVE as a group and on your own.

THE 4 S'S OF GOOD OBSERVATION

1 STRUCTURE	**Look at the passage as a whole.**	Biographical, historical, geographical, chronological, logical, or ideological? Whose POV is it written from? What phrases or clauses seem to go together? How are the sentences connected to make paragraphs or sections? Are there "connector" words at the beginning/end of the passage?
2 SHAPE	**In what form did the writer choose to write? Is there . . .**	Comparison or contrast? Cause and effect? Interrogation? Repetition? Explanation or an analysis? Narrative? Argument? Summary? A move from general to specific? (Or specific to general?) Unity or continuity? A pivot?
3 SPEECH	**Look at the parts of speech used by the writer—specific terms, words, choices, etc.**	Are there any unusual terms? Do any terms used make you wonder about the translation from the original language? Which words are figurative vs. literal? Which words are most crucial to the passage? Which words represent a climax or a shift? Are any words in contrast or opposition to each other? Do any terms appear in a list? Are there proper nouns or names?
4 SENSE	**Observe the mood and atmosphere created by the people, situations and words.**	What words indicate a tone of the writer or speaker? What terms or phrases used conjure or communicate a feeling? What is the mood of the section or situation in which it appears?

Turn the page for the During-Video Group Practice.

Leader, read this prayer aloud before reading the passage to the group.

Holy Spirit, we invite You into this space and time as we open Your Word. Father God, we seek to know and understand You and Your Word more fully. Lead us and show us what You intend to reveal for us. In Jesus' name, *Amen*

Read this passage and note your OBSERVATIONS briefly, then discuss the questions as a group on the following page for a short experience of practicing OBSERVATION.

Genesis 48:1–6

OBSERVATION NOTES

Some time later Joseph was told, "Your father is ill." So he took his two sons Manasseh and Ephraim along with him. When Jacob was told, "Your son Joseph has come to you," Israel rallied his strength and sat up on the bed.

Jacob said to Joseph, "God Almighty appeared to me at Luz in the land of Canaan, and there he blessed me and said to me, 'I am going to make you fruitful and increase your numbers. I will make you a community of peoples, and I will give this land as an everlasting possession to your descendants after you.'

"Now then, your two sons born to you in Egypt before I came to you here will be reckoned as mine; Ephraim and Manasseh will be mine, just as Reuben and Simeon are mine. Any children born to you after them will be yours; in the territory they inherit they will be reckoned under the names of their brothers."

- Share your top few OBSERVATIONS out loud as a group.

- Give each other feedback: Did everyone stick to only what you can see in the text?

- Discuss any themes you saw/heard.

- Discuss any truths you can take away from this passage.

TIME'S UP!

Return now to the video for a short wrap-up of this practice from Alli.

GROUP DISCUSSION

Leader, read each prompt to the group for deeper discussion. Do not be concerned if you don't make it through every question. Trust the Spirit to lead your discussion where and how your group needs to connect and grow.

1. In what contexts or situations do you practice OBSERVATION in your daily life? Are there specific circumstances that cause you to pay closer attention?

2. Have you ever asked the Holy Spirit to join you in your personal Bible study or reading time? If so, what changes have you noticed when you do? If not, what could make you more confident in asking for His presence?

3. What was your experience with OBSERVATION in Bible study before today?

4. What about this practice intrigued you most and why? What challenged you and why?

5. Alli noted that OBSERVATION requires humility—a willingness to let go of what you thought you understood in order to learn even more. Discuss as a group how you might prevent bringing preconceived notions of Scripture into your study time.

6. If the Spirit leads your practice of OBSERVATION, how might that change your experience of reading the Bible?

7. In our group practice, how did OBSERVATION through Genesis 48:1–6 sharpen, deepen, or change your understanding of . . .

- God?
- Yourself or humanity?
- Living a life of faith?

PREP FOR INDIVIDUAL PRACTICE

Leader, read this instruction about personal practice between meetings to the group.

This week you will read three passages of Scripture on your own and practice OBSERVATION.

On the following pages you will find a handy reference chart for How-To Practice: OBSERVATION. I encourage you to dive into this practice with your whole heart and ask the Holy Spirit to reveal something new and edifying to you as you do!

CLOSING PRAYER

Leader, read this prayer over your group before dismissing.

Lord thank You for Your timeless Word that is able to reveal new layers of truth and grace every time we observe it. Open our eyes and hearts by Your Spirit so that we can receive more of You as we read. Give us patience and endurance to slow down and soak in all that You have left for us to discover. In Jesus' name,

Amen

HOW-TO PRACTICE: OBSERVATION

1 STRUCTURE	**Look at the passage as a whole.**	Biographical, historical, geographical, chronological, logical, or ideological? Whose POV is it written from? What phrases or clauses seem to go together? How are the sentences connected to make paragraphs or sections? Are there "connector" words at the beginning/end of the passage?
2 PRACTICE	**In what form did the writer choose to write?** **Is there . . .**	Comparison or contrast? Cause and effect? Interrogation? Repetition? Explanation or an analysis? Narrative? Argument? Summary? A move from general to specific? (Or specific to general?) Unity or continuity? A pivot?

3 **SPEECH**	**Look at the parts of speech used by the writer—specific terms, word choices, etc.**	Are there any unusual terms? Do any terms used make you wonder about the translation from the original language? Which words are figurative vs. literal? Which words are most crucial to the passage? Which words represent a climax or a shift? Are any words in contrast or opposition to each other? Do any terms appear in a list? Are there proper nouns or names? Identify: nouns, pronouns, verbs/tenses, adjectives, adverbs, prepositions, person, voice, tone, etc.

4 **SENSE**	**Observe the mood and atmosphere created by the people, situations, and words.**	What words indicate a tone of the writer or speaker? What terms or phrases used conjure or communicate a feeling? What is the mood of the section or situation in which it appears?

HOW-TO PRACTICE: OBSERVATION

Example Observations of a Passage

In this study, we will observe within a paragraph/passage of Scripture because it's the most helpful unit in which to practice. However, just to give you a few examples of good vs. bad observations I've used just one verse to demonstrate the idea:

Hebrews 4:13

> Nothing in all creation is hidden from God's sight. Everything is uncovered and laid bare before the eyes of him to whom we must give account.

GOOD OBSERVATIONS	BAD OBSERVATIONS
Nothing and *everything* are opposite terms, forming a contrast within the verse and between the sentences. This contrast continues and emphasizes the same idea.	You can't hide things from God. *(This might be true but it is also a conclusion of personal implications—not an observation of the words. This will be best discussed as you talk about truths/themes.)*
The second sentence contains an explanation of the uncovering (to "give account").	I'll have to tell God everything I did. *(This assumes you're part of the "we"—need further investigation of context to say for sure. The method of giving account is not stated. Perhaps do more investigation of the term give account to know if it indicates speech.)*
Uncovered and *laid bare* are similar terms repeating the same idea. Both are the opposite of *hidden*, creating another contrast in the verse.	God will call you out for what you do. (*This is an assumption of God's behavior that goes beyond what is stated here.*)
Is is a present-tense verb that indicates action that is happening now.	One day I'll stand before God. (*The verse does not say anything about "standing." It also does not say it is in the future, which may be an understanding you have from somewhere else.*)
Must give is an imperative indicating a requirement: The account is not optional.	God's eyes and sight are metaphorical. *(There is nothing in this particular verse to indicate that; this assumption or knowledge does not come from this verse.)*

SESSION 1

OBSERVATION

INDIVIDUAL PRACTICE

Now it's time to try the practice of OBSERVATION on your own.

Don't worry if it feels slow or a little clunky for now. Take all the time you need to read and explore these ten verses from the book of Exodus and practice making great observations. You'll bring these back to your next group meeting, so be sure to do this before the next time you meet!

OBSERVATION PRACTICE Day 1

Pray. Read the Scripture passage. Note your OBSERVATIONS as you read. Answer the questions and fill out the OBSERVATION practice worksheet on the following pages. Refer back to the HOW-TO PRACTICE: OBSERVATION on pages 22–24 for more guidance if needed.

Exodus 3:1–10

Now Moses was tending the flock of Jethro his father-in-law, the priest of Midian, and he led the flock to the far side of the wilderness and came to Horeb, the mountain of God. There the angel of the LORD appeared to him in flames of fire from within a bush. Moses saw that though the bush was on fire it did not burn up. So Moses thought, "I will go over and see this strange sight—why the bush does not burn up."

When the LORD saw that he had gone over to look, God called to him from within the bush, "Moses! Moses!"

OBSERVATION NOTES

And Moses said, "Here I am."

"Do not come any closer," God said. "Take off your sandals, for the place where you are standing is holy ground." Then he said, "I am the God of your father, the God of Abraham, the God of Isaac and the God of Jacob." At this, Moses hid his face, because he was afraid to look at God.

The LORD said, "I have indeed seen the misery of my people in Egypt. I have heard them crying out because of their slave drivers, and I am concerned about their suffering. So I have come down to rescue them from the hand of the Egyptians and to bring them up out of that land into a good and spacious land, a land flowing with milk and honey—the home of the Canaanites, Hittites, Amorites, Perizzites, Hivites and Jebusites. And now the cry of the Israelites has reached me, and I have seen the way the Egyptians are oppressing them. So now, go. I am sending you to Pharaoh to bring my people the Israelites out of Egypt."

What are a few immediate observations you had as you read this passage?

Read the passage again.

Write down three to five more observations using the 4 S's on the next page.

4 S'S OF OBSERVATION

1 STRUCTURE	Look at the passage as a whole.	
2 SHAPE	In what form did the writer choose to write? Is there . . .	
3 SPEECH	Look at the parts of speech used by the writer—specific terms, words, choices, etc.	
4 SENSE	Observe the mood and atmosphere created by the people, situations, and words.	

Look back at the observations you wrote down:

What are the ***themes*** within your observations?

What are the ***truths*** you can take away from your observations?

How did OBSERVATION through Exodus 3:1–10 sharpen, deepen, or change your understanding of . . .

- God?
- Yourself or humanity?
- Living a life of faith?

OBSERVATION PRACTICE Day 2

Pray. Read the Scripture passage. Note your OBSERVATIONS as you read. Answer the questions and fill out the OBSERVATION practice worksheet on the following pages. Refer back to the HOW-TO PRACTICE: OBSERVATION on pages 22–24 for more guidance if needed.

Hebrews 2:1–9	OBSERVATION NOTES

We must pay the most careful attention, therefore, to what we have heard, so that we do not drift away. For since the message spoken through angels was binding, and every violation and disobedience received its just punishment, how shall we escape if we ignore so great a salvation? This salvation, which was first announced by the Lord, was confirmed to us by those who heard him. God also testified to it by signs, wonders and various miracles, and by gifts of the Holy Spirit distributed according to his will. It is not to angels that he has subjected the world to come, about which we are speaking. But there is a place where someone has testified:

"What is mankind that you are mindful of them, a son of man that you care for him?

You made them a little lower than the angels; you crowned them with glory and honor and put everything under their feet."

In putting everything under them, God left nothing that is not subject to them. Yet at present we do not see everything subject to them. But we do see Jesus, who was made lower than the angels for a little while, now crowned with glory and honor because he suffered death, so that by the grace of God he might taste death for everyone.

What are a few immediate observations you had as you read this passage?

Read the passage again.

Write down three to five more observations using the 4 S's on the next page.

4 S'S OF OBSERVATION

1 STRUCTURE	Look at the passage as a whole.	
2 SHAPE	In what form did the writer choose to write? Is there . . .	
3 SPEECH	Look at the parts of speech used by the writer—specific terms, words, choices, etc.	
4 SENSE	Observe the mood and atmosphere created by the people, situations, and words.	

Look back at the observations you wrote down:

What are the ***themes*** within your observations?

What are the ***truths*** you can take away from your observations?

How did OBSERVATION through Hebrews 2:1–9 sharpen, deepen, or change your understanding of . . .

- God?
- Yourself or humanity?
- Living a life of faith?

OBSERVATION PRACTICE Day 3

Pray. Read the Scripture passage. Note your OBSERVATIONS as you read. Answer the questions and fill out the OBSERVATION practice worksheet on the following pages. Refer back to the HOW TO PRACTICE: OBSERVATION on pages 22–24 for more guidance if needed.

Esther 2:1–7

OBSERVATION NOTES

Later when King Xerxes' fury had subsided, he remembered Vashti and what she had done and what he had decreed about her. Then the king's personal attendants proposed, "Let a search be made for beautiful young virgins for the king. Let the king appoint commissioners in every province of his realm to bring all these beautiful young women into the harem at the citadel of Susa. Let them be placed under the care of Hegai, the king's eunuch, who is in charge of the women; and let beauty treatments be given to them. Then let the young woman who pleases the king be queen instead of Vashti." This advice appealed to the king, and he followed it.

Now there was in the citadel of Susa a Jew of the tribe of Benjamin, named Mordecai son of Jair, the son of Shimei, the son of Kish, who had been carried into exile from Jerusalem by Nebuchadnezzar king of Babylon, among those taken captive with Jehoiachin king of Judah. Mordecai had a cousin named Hadassah, whom he had brought up because she had neither father nor mother. This young woman, who was also known as Esther, had a lovely figure and was beautiful. Mordecai had taken her as his own daughter when her father and mother died.

What are a few immediate observations you had as you read this passage?

Read the passage again.

Write down three to five more observations using the 4 S's on the next page.

4 S'S OF OBSERVATION

1 STRUCTURE	Look at the passage as a whole.	
2 SHAPE	In what form did the writer choose to write? Is there . . .	
3 SPEECH	Look at the parts of speech used by the writer—specific terms, words, choices, etc.	
4 SENSE	Observe the mood and atmosphere created by the people, situations, and words.	

Look back at the observations you wrote down:

What are the ***themes*** within your observations?

What are the ***truths*** you can take away from your observations?

How did OBSERVATION through Esther 2:1–7 sharpen, deepen, or change your understanding of . . .

- God?
- Yourself or humanity?
- Living a life of faith?

Great work!
I hope OBSERVATION will become the very foundation of your time inside the Bible.

SESSION 2

LISTENING

GROUP MEETING

Leader, read aloud to the group.

Welcome to *Spirit-Led Bible Study* Session 2!

Session 1 was focused on what you can see with your eyes on the pages of Scripture, while Session 2 is all about your ears.

The practice of LISTENING requires the use of both your physical and spiritual ears.

Throughout the Bible, the practice of LISTENING is associated with the voice of the Spirit and wisdom from God. This is what we seek through this practice. The same sentence is written seven times in the book of Revelation (2:7, 11, 17, 29; 3:6, 13, 22). Think of it as your call to begin this new practice.

"Whoever has ears, let them hear what the Spirit says to the churches."

Romans 3:22

REVIEW SESSION 1 INDIVIDUAL PRACTICE

Leader, read these instructions aloud to the group before you begin. I recommend setting a ten-minute timer so you don't spend too long here; you'll need most of your group time for the new practice of LISTENING!

Refer to your OBSERVATION Day 1 Individual Practice on pages 27–31 to review your homework as a group.

Share one or two of your best OBSERVATIONS from Exodus 3:1–10. Record your group's list in the box below.

What themes stand out from the OBSERVATIONS of your whole group?

What is the one obvious biblical truth you can agree to take away from Exodus 3:1–10?

OUR SHARED BIBLICAL TRUTH:

____

Share briefly one of the ways OBSERVATION through Exodus 3:1–10 sharpened, deepened, or changed your understanding of . . .

- God.
- Yourself or humanity.
- Living a life of faith.

Now it's time to begin our next *Spirit-Led Bible Study* practice!
Turn the page for the warm-up exercise.

WARM-UP

Leader, set a five-minute timer. Share the instructions below with the group and carry on reading below when the time expires.

During this time there is absolutely no talking. All you are going to do is LISTEN.

Write down any sounds you hear.

TIME'S UP!

Consider which sounds were loud and obvious and which ones were more subtle.

Is there anything you hadn't even realized was there? Did anyone close their eyes to try to hear better?

Did it help?

Hold on to what you just learned.

WORD OF ENCOURAGEMENT FROM ALLI

Leader, read this aloud or select a volunteer to read to the group.

When my four kids were young toddlers, there were days the unending jabber was just too much for me to follow. I tried hard to pay attention, but often toddlers don't make a lot of sense! I know it's important for speech development, so I didn't want them to stop—I just didn't have the capacity to LISTEN to every word. If you have ever been around a toddler, you know what I mean. LISTENING takes a lot of energy! So I developed a fake version. I actually had a tactic to feign real LISTENING. I would simply repeat back their last two (intelligible) words in a nice tone of voice. It went something like this...

Toddler: "blah blah blah blah blah my dump truck."
Me: "Dump truck . . . sounds great, sweetie" or "Dump truck . . . what color?"

I had absolutely no idea what had actually been said, but it sure seemed like I did.

This is how a lot of us read the Bible. We read the words on the page, get the general idea, and take a quick note of a key word or two and move on, not truly expecting or LISTENING for the voice of God within the words. The Spirit is speaking to you in, around, and through Scripture. You—personally! We are too content with a fleeting glimpse and a couple of summary words when there is so much more! Jesus said, "My sheep listen to my voice; I know them, and they follow me" (John 10:27). If you want a life following Jesus as your personal Shepherd, LISTENING to His voice is a key practice. The Word of God is speaking. Instead of settling into a shallower version, use this session to help you practice deeply, with the expectation that you will hear His voice!

NOW IT'S TIME TO TURN ON THE SESSION 2 VIDEO.

WATCH SESSION 2 VIDEO

Leader, stream the video or play the DVD.

LISTENING PRACTICE NOTES

This practice doesn't depend on new information. Use this section for space to take notes on what you hear throughout the video teaching.

LISTENING

LISTEN BEFORE you open your Bible.

- What emotions am I "hearing" loudly within me today?
- What thoughts are on repeat inside my head?
- What do I hear in the environment around me?
- What is the last thing I "heard" from God?

LISTEN DURING your reading of the Bible.

- What words are still ringing in my ears?
- What parts of the passage were unwelcome or sounded like a clanging in my ears?
- How or why might these clanging words connect with my life right now?

LISTEN FOR WHAT THE SPIRIT MIGHT BE SAYING TO YOU IN ENCOURAGEMENT OR WARNING OR CONVICTION.

(10 MINUTES)

DURING-VIDEO GROUP PRACTICE

Leader, invite the Holy Spirit into your group time and read the following instructions and prompts to the group as you engage in this practice.

LISTEN BEFORE YOU OPEN YOUR BIBLE. (1 MINUTE)

Take a moment to ask yourself these questions. LISTEN for one full minute. Make notes in the box provided on any thoughts, images, or fleeting words.

- What emotions am I "hearing" loudly within me today?
- What thoughts are on repeat inside my head?
- What do I hear in the environment around me?
- What is the last thing I "heard" from God?

DURING-VIDEO GROUP PRACTICE

LISTEN <u>DURING</u> YOUR READING OF THE BIBLE. (4 MINUTES)

Leader, select one person to read Psalm 131 out loud or play it from an audio Bible on your phone. Then read the prompts aloud and encourage your group to fill in the boxes before you return to the video.

Psalm 131

A song of ascents. Of David.

My heart is not proud, LORD,
my eyes are not haughty;
I do not concern myself with great matters
or things too wonderful for me.
But I have calmed and quieted myself,
I am like a weaned child with its mother;
like a weaned child I am content.

Israel, put your hope in the LORD
both now and forevermore.

Have someone else read Psalm 131 one more time, out loud, in **a different translation** (any one you choose!). If you do not have another one available, here's *The Message* translation:

Psalm 131 MSG

GOD, I'm not trying to rule the roost,
I don't want to be king of the mountain.
I haven't meddled where I have no business
or fantasized grandiose plans.
I've kept my feet on the ground,
I've cultivated a quiet heart.
Like a baby content in its mother's arms,
my soul is a baby content.
Wait, Israel, for GOD. Wait with hope.
Hope now; hope always!

Record what you heard on the next page.

What words are still ringing in your ears right now?

Share with your group the part that reverberated the loudest. What words/parts of this psalm were unwelcome or clanging in your ears?

Share with your group the most unappealing/chafing part to you. How or why might these words connect to your life right now?

Write down what the Spirit might be saying to you personally.

TIME'S UP!

Return now to the video for a short wrap-up of this practice from Alli.

GROUP DISCUSSION

Leader, read each prompt to the group for deeper discussion. Do not be concerned if you don't make it through every question. Trust the Spirit to lead your discussion where and how your group needs to connect and grow.

1. Take turns sharing out loud what you think the Spirit is saying to you. (Remember, your group is there as a filter to affirm, challenge, or question the voice of God in your life. Give each other permission to speak openly and honestly.)

2. What was your experience with LISTENING in Bible study before today? What about this practice intrigued you most and why? What challenged you and why?

3. Is there something in your life that you understand better as a result of what you heard from the Spirit in your LISTENING practice today? (Again, use your group as a sounding board to discuss and affirm options.)

4. Alli noted, "It can be tricky to hear and to separate [the Holy Spirit's] voice from the noise around us . . . (and) inside our own heads. The communication of the Spirit is a holy interruption to this noise, not part of it." As a group, discuss ways to help turn down the noise around you every day. What might help you hear the voice of God?

5. Alli shared that the Word of God and the people of God prevent you from being misled in what you believe is the voice of God. Discuss how you might go about checking what you believe you have heard in Scripture. How can you, as a group, become partners for one another as you practice LISTENING to the Spirit?

6. How did the practice of LISTENING to Psalm 131 sharpen, deepen, or change your understanding of . . .

   - God?
   - Yourself or humanity?
   - Living a life of faith?

PREP FOR INDIVIDUAL STUDY

Leader, read this to the group.

This week you will read multiple passages of Scripture on your own and practice LISTENING. On the following pages, you will find a handy reference chart for how to practice LISTENING well. I encourage you to dive into this practice with your whole heart and ask the Holy Spirit to reveal something new and edifying to you as you do!

CLOSING PRAYER

Leader, read this prayer over your group before dismissing.

Jesus, thank You for being the living Word of God and wanting to speak personally to each of us. Help us to hear Your voice loudly and to be courageous enough to receive it and follow You. In Jesus' name,

Amen

HOW-TO PRACTICE: LISTENING

1. **FIND A QUIET, UNDISTURBED PLACE.** Pause. Breathe. Invite the Holy Spirit into your Bible study.
2. **LISTEN BEFORE YOU OPEN YOUR BIBLE.** Ask yourself these questions and record your responses in a journal or your workbook pages (wherever you are recording your Bible study learnings).

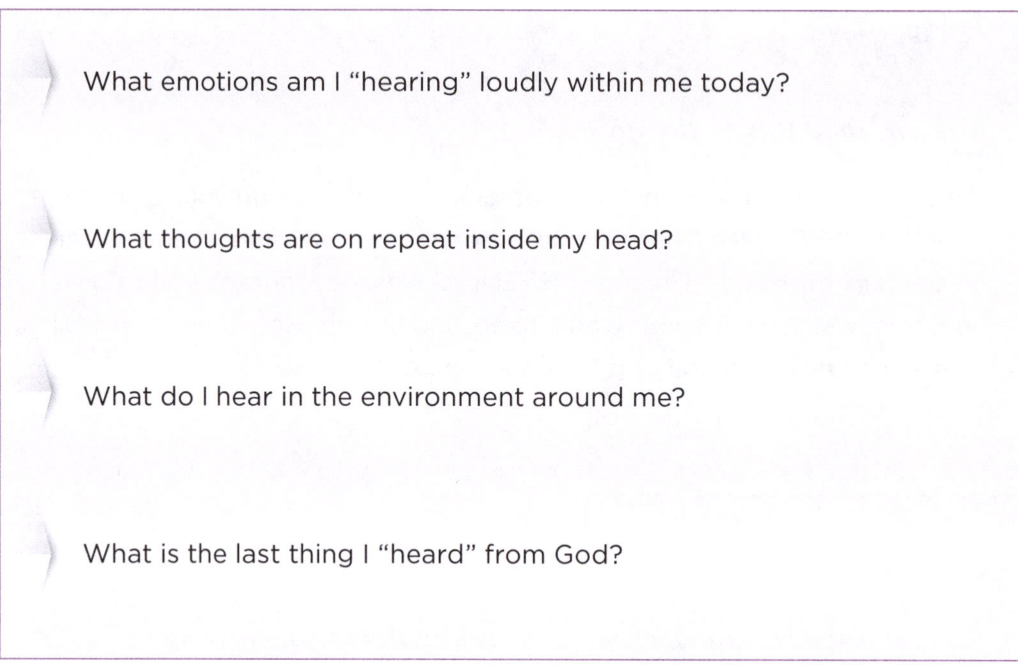

- What emotions am I "hearing" loudly within me today?
- What thoughts are on repeat inside my head?
- What do I hear in the environment around me?
- What is the last thing I "heard" from God?

3. **LISTEN DURING YOUR READING OF THE BIBLE.** Then, notice and record your responses to what you heard.

- What words are still ringing in your ears right now?

- What words/parts of this passage were unwelcome or clanging in your ears?

- How or why might these words connect to your life right now?

SESSION 2

LISTENING

INDIVIDUAL PRACTICE

Now it's time to try the practice of LISTENING on your own. Don't worry if LISTENING doesn't come naturally to you. Statistically, people have over four thousand words going through their minds per minute. Learning how to LISTEN to God is just that: learned. Which means LISTENING takes practice.

Be patient with yourself. Perhaps take a few deep breaths to relax, and invite the Holy Spirit to silence all the noise so that you can hear His voice and whatever He intends to bring to mind.

Don't be shy about recording where this practice presented a challenge or difficulty. When you share with your group in your next meeting, your experience may be similar to someone else's. Your honesty might just give another person the confidence to try again.

LISTENING PRACTICE Day 1

1. LISTEN *before* you open your Bible.

Ask yourself the following questions. Take one minute of silence to LISTEN. Then, record your notes of any thoughts, images, or fleeting words you hear.

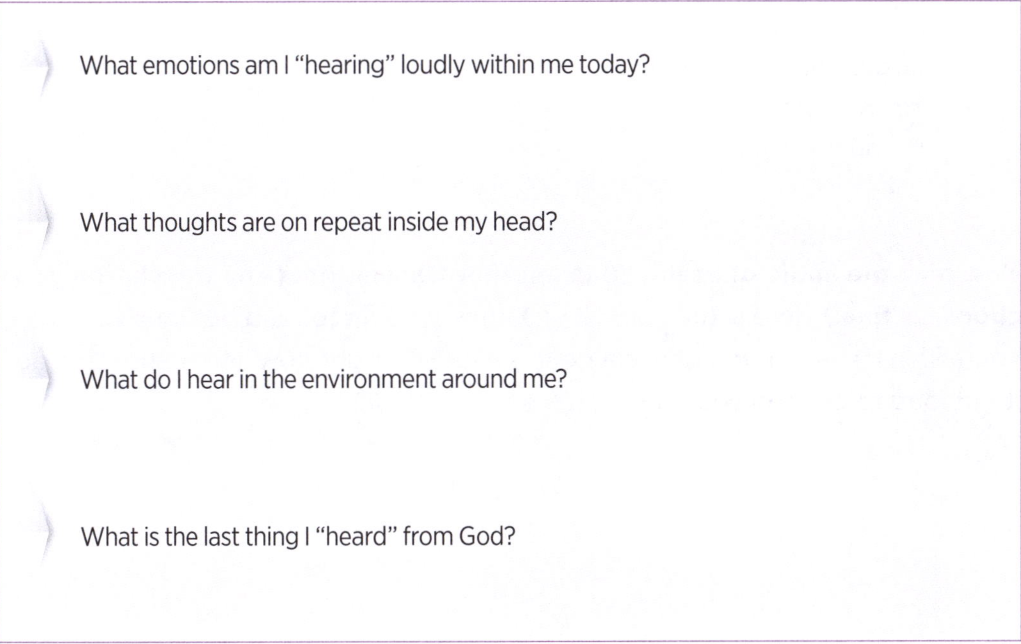

What emotions am I "hearing" loudly within me today?

What thoughts are on repeat inside my head?

What do I hear in the environment around me?

What is the last thing I "heard" from God?

Play the audio version of Psalm 70 using a Bible app on your phone or computer. If you cannot LISTEN on a device, read the psalm out loud to yourself.

Psalm 70

For the director of music. Of David. A petition.

Hasten, O God, to save me;
  come quickly, LORD, to help me.

May those who want to take my life
  be put to shame and confusion;
may all who desire my ruin
  be turned back in disgrace.
May those who say to me, "Aha! Aha!"
  turn back because of their shame.
But may all who seek you
  rejoice and be glad in you;
may those who long for your saving help always say,
  "The LORD is great!"

But as for me, I am poor and needy;
  come quickly to me, O God.
You are my help and my deliverer;
  LORD, do not delay.

Now play the audio of Psalm 70 in another translation. (Any translation you choose is fine.) Here is the New King James Version to read out loud to yourself in case you don't have a device with you right now. Make sure to read it out loud to engage your ears!

Psalm 70 NKJV

Prayer for Relief from Adversaries
To the Chief Musician. A Psalm of David. To bring to remembrance.
Make haste, O God, to deliver me!
Make haste to help me, O LORD!
Let them be ashamed and confounded
Who seek my life;
Let them be turned back and confused
Who desire my hurt.
Let them be turned back because of their shame,
Who say, "Aha, aha!"
Let all those who seek You rejoice and be glad in You;
And let those who love Your salvation say continually,
"Let God be magnified!"
But I am poor and needy;
Make haste to me, O God!
You are my help and my deliverer;
O LORD, do not delay.

What words are still ringing in your ears right now?

Commit to taking these words with you into your day.
LISTEN for them throughout your day.

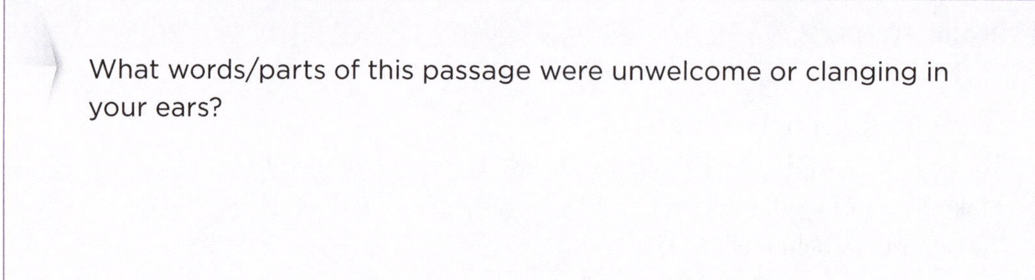

What words/parts of this passage were unwelcome or clanging in your ears?

Pay attention to this! The Holy Spirit uses unwelcome or clanging words or sounds as a tactic to push you to learn, to clarify, and to investigate whatever it is that is unsettling in your spirit. Ask Him for help. Seek discernment. Spend a few minutes LISTENING a bit more.

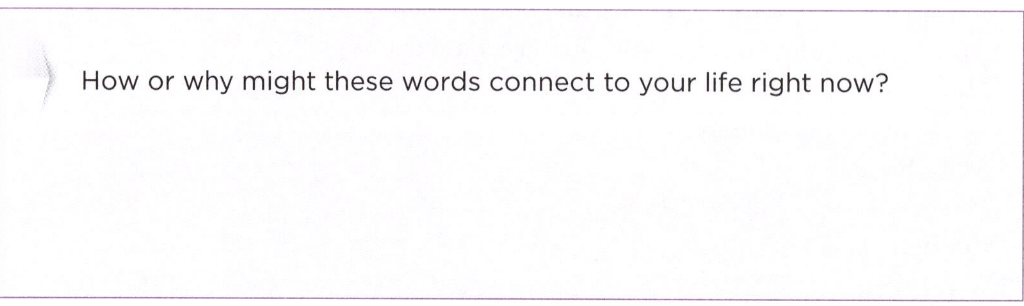

How or why might these words connect to your life right now?

LISTEN for something the Holy Spirit might be saying to you personally, directly, or specifically.

How did the practice of LISTENING to Psalm 70 deepen or alter your understanding of . . .

- God?
- Yourself or humanity?
- Living a life of faith?

LISTENING PRACTICE Day 2

1. LISTEN *before* you open your Bible.

Ask yourself the following questions. Take one minute of silence to LISTEN. Take notes of any thoughts, images, or fleeting words you hear.

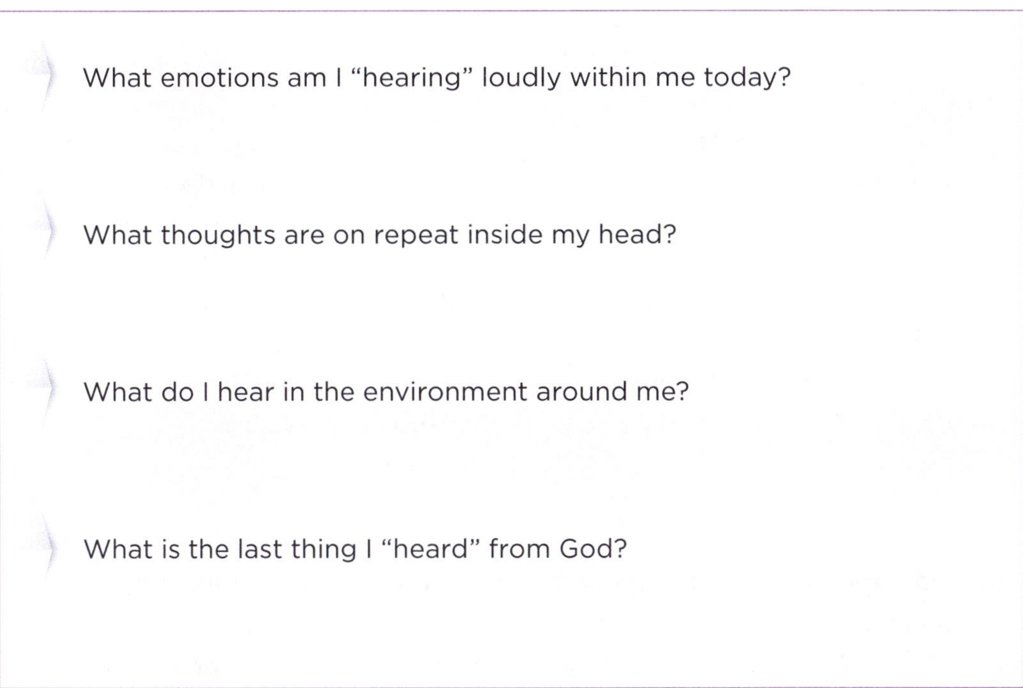

2. LISTEN *during* your reading of the Bible.

Play the audio version of Philippians 2:1–11 using a Bible app on your phone or computer. If you cannot LISTEN on a device, read the passage out loud to yourself.

Philippians 2:1–11

Therefore if you have any encouragement from being united with Christ, if any comfort from his love, if any common sharing in the Spirit, if any tenderness and compassion, then make my joy complete by being like-minded, having the same love, being one in spirit and of one mind. Do nothing out of selfish ambition or vain conceit. Rather, in humility value others above yourselves, not looking to your own interests but each of you to the interests of the others. In your relationships with one another, have the same mindset as Christ Jesus: Who, being in very nature God, did not consider equality with God something to be used to his own advantage; rather, he made himself nothing by taking the very nature of a servant, being made in human likeness. And being found in appearance as a man, he humbled himself by becoming obedient to death—even death on a cross! Therefore God exalted him to the highest place and gave him the name that is above every name, that at the name of Jesus every knee should bow, in heaven and on earth and under the earth, and every tongue acknowledge that Jesus Christ is Lord, to the glory of God the Father.

Now, play the audio of Philippians 2:1–11 in another translation. (Any translation you choose is fine.) Here is the New American Standard Bible to read out loud to yourself in case you don't have a device with you right now. Make sure to read it out loud to engage your ears!

Philippians 2:1–11 NASB

Therefore if there is any encouragement in Christ, if any consolation of love, if any fellowship of the Spirit, if any affection and compassion, make my joy complete by being of the same mind, maintaining the same love, united in spirit, intent on one purpose. Do nothing from selfishness or empty conceit, but with humility consider one another as more important than yourselves; do not merely look out for your own personal interests, but also for the interests of others. Have this attitude in yourselves which was also in Christ Jesus, who, as He already existed in the form of God, did not consider equality with God something to be grasped, but emptied Himself by taking the form of a bond-servant and being born in the likeness of men. And being found in appearance as a man, He humbled Himself by becoming obedient to the point of death: death on a cross. For this reason also God highly exalted Him, and bestowed on Him the name which is above every name, so that at the name of Jesus EVERY KNEE WILL BOW, of those who are in heaven and on earth and under the earth, and that every tongue will confess that Jesus Christ is Lord, to the glory of God the Father.

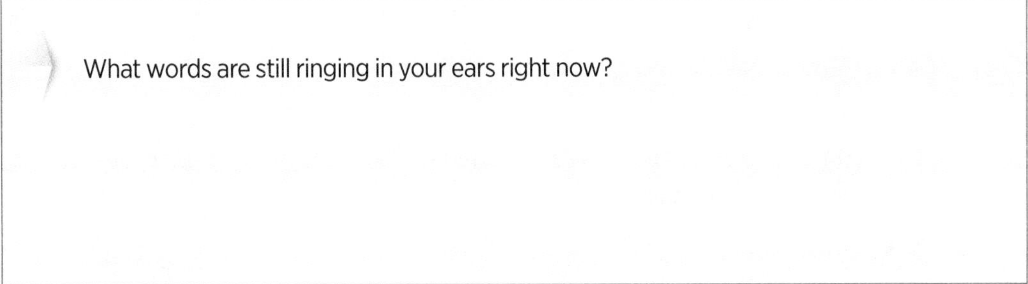

What words are still ringing in your ears right now?

Commit to taking these words with you into your day.
LISTEN for them throughout your day.

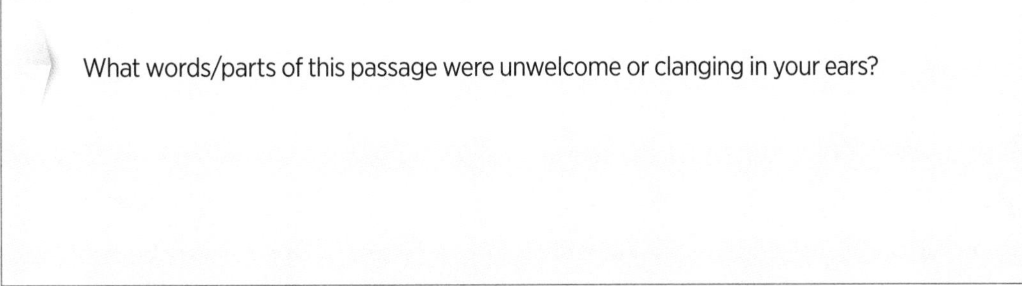

What words/parts of this passage were unwelcome or clanging in your ears?

Pay attention to this! The Holy Spirit uses unwelcome or clanging words or sounds as a tactic to push you to learn, to clarify, and to investigate whatever it is that is unsettling in your spirit. Ask Him for help. Seek discernment. Spend a few minutes LISTENING a bit more.

How or why might these words connect to your life right now?

LISTEN for something the Holy Spirit might be saying to you personally, directly, or specifically.

How did the practice of LISTENING to Philippians 2:1–11 deepen or alter your understanding of . . .

- God?
- Yourself or humanity?
- Living a life of faith?

LISTENING PRACTICE Day 3

1. LISTEN *before* you open the Bible.

Ask yourself the following questions. Take one minute of silence to LISTEN. Take notes of any thoughts, images, or fleeting words you hear.

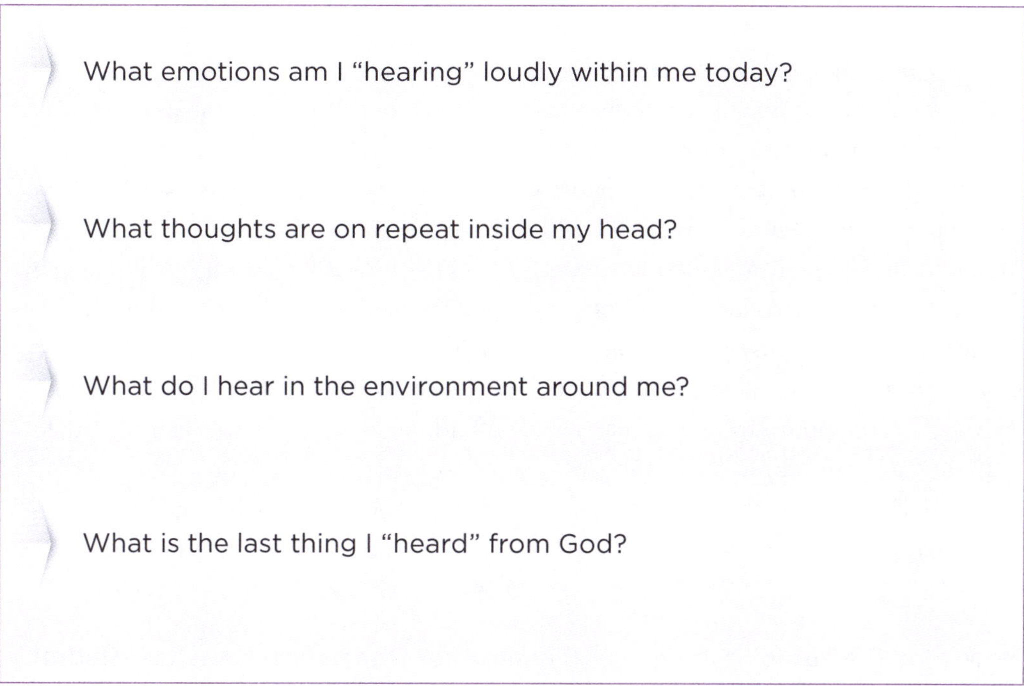

- What emotions am I "hearing" loudly within me today?
- What thoughts are on repeat inside my head?
- What do I hear in the environment around me?
- What is the last thing I "heard" from God?

2. LISTEN *during* your reading of the Bible.

Play the audio version of John 13:1–11 using a Bible app on your phone or computer. If you cannot LISTEN on a device, read the passage out loud to yourself.

John 13:1–11

It was just before the Passover Festival. Jesus knew that the hour had come for him to leave this world and go to the Father. Having loved his own who were in the world, he loved them to the end.

The evening meal was in progress, and the devil had already prompted Judas, the son of Simon Iscariot, to betray Jesus. Jesus knew that the Father had put all things under his power, and that he had come from God and was returning to God; so he got up from the meal, took off his outer clothing, and wrapped a towel around his waist. After that, he poured water into a basin and began to wash his disciples' feet, drying them with the towel that was wrapped around him.

He came to Simon Peter, who said to him, "Lord, are you going to wash my feet?"

Jesus replied, "You do not realize now what I am doing, but later you will understand."

"No," said Peter, "you shall never wash my feet."

Jesus answered, "Unless I wash you, you have no part with me."

"Then, Lord," Simon Peter replied, "not just my feet but my hands and my head as well!"

Jesus answered, "Those who have had a bath need only to wash their feet; their whole body is clean. And you are clean, though not every one of you." For he knew who was going to betray him, and that was why he said not every one was clean.

Now, play the audio of John 13:1–11 in another translation. (Any translation you choose is fine.) Here is the New Living Translation to read out loud to yourself in case you don't have a device with you right now. Make sure to read it out loud to engage your ears!

John 13:1–11 NLT

Before the Passover celebration, Jesus knew that his hour had come to leave this world and return to his Father. He had loved his disciples during his ministry on earth, and now he loved them to the very end. It was time for supper, and the devil had already prompted Judas, son of Simon Iscariot, to betray Jesus. Jesus knew that the Father had given him authority over everything and that he had come from God and would return to God. So he got up from the table, took off his robe, wrapped a towel around his waist, and poured water into a basin. Then he began to wash the disciples' feet, drying them with the towel he had around him.

When Jesus came to Simon Peter, Peter said to him, "Lord, are you going to wash my feet?"

Jesus replied, "You don't understand now what I am doing, but someday you will."

"No," Peter protested, "you will never ever wash my feet!"

Jesus replied, "Unless I wash you, you won't belong to me."

Simon Peter exclaimed, "Then wash my hands and head as well, Lord, not just my feet!"

Jesus replied, "A person who has bathed all over does not need to wash, except for the feet, to be entirely clean. And you disciples are clean, but not all of you." For Jesus knew who would betray him. That is what he meant when he said, "Not all of you are clean."

What words are still ringing in your ears right now?

Commit to taking these words with you into your day.
LISTEN for them throughout your day.

What words/parts of this passage were unwelcome or clanging in your ears?

Pay attention to this! The Holy Spirit uses unwelcome or clanging words or sounds as a tactic to push you to learn, to clarify, and to investigate whatever it is that is unsettling in your spirit. Ask Him for help. Seek discernment. Spend a few minutes LISTENING a bit more.

How or why might these words connect to your life right now?

LISTEN for something the Holy Spirit might be saying to you personally, directly, or specifically.

How did the practice of LISTENING to John 13:1–11 deepen or alter your understanding of . . .

- God?
- Yourself or humanity?
- Living a life of faith?

Great work.
You have two new tools in your Bible study tool box!

SESSION 3

ORIENTATION

GROUP MEETING

Leader, read aloud to the group.

Welcome to *Spirit-Led Bible Study* Session 3: ORIENTATION.

This practice is about going back to three very basic questions that will set your mind and heart straight, helping you properly understand anything you read in the Bible. What seem like simple, foundational pieces of information (and they are!) will not only help you grasp the story taking place throughout all of Scripture but also reveal God's character and plans in very surprising ways!

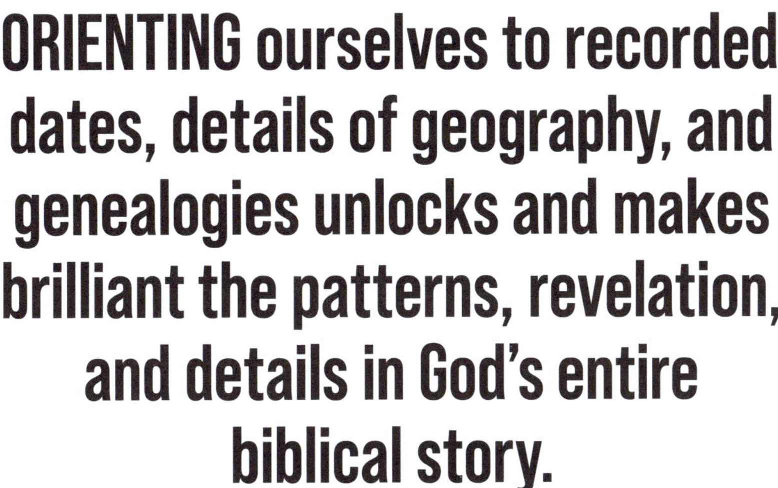

> As the sailor locates his position on the sea by "shooting" the sun, so we may get our moral bearings by looking at God. We must begin with God. We are right when and only when we stand in a right position relative to God, and we are wrong so far and so long as we stand in any other position.
>
> **A. W. Tozer, *The Pursuit of God***

REVIEW SESSION 2 INDIVIDUAL PRACTICE

Leader, read these instructions aloud to the group before you begin. I recommend setting a ten-minute timer so you don't spend too much time here; you'll need most of your group time for the new practice of ORIENTATION.

In Session 2 you used your ears to hear Psalm 70 to LISTEN to the voice of the Holy Spirit. Let's review what we learned while speaking openly and honestly as a strong filter for each other. Refer to LISTENING Day 1 Individual Practice on pages 57–60 to review your homework as a group.

Take turns sharing one thing you think the Spirit was saying to you in your LISTENING practice this past week. (Remember, your group is there as a filter to affirm, challenge, or question the voice of God in your life.)

What part of your life is clearer as a result of what you heard from the Spirit in your LISTENING practice last week?

What is the one obvious biblical truth you can agree to take away from Psalm 70?

OUR SHARED BIBLICAL TRUTH:

Briefly, what is one way the practice of LISTENING to Psalm 70 sharpened, deepened, or changed your understanding of . . .

- God?
- Yourself or humanity?
- Living a life of faith?

Now it's time to begin our next *Spirit-Led Bible Study* practice!

WARM-UP

Leader, set a five-minute timer. Share the instructions below with the group.

TELL YOUR STORY ON A MAP

- Place dots on the map to represent all the places you have lived. Draw a line connecting them in order of when you lived where. If you have lived outside the US, draw that in too.
- Take turns sharing your maps with one another.
- Talk very briefly about the length of time you were in each place and what took you to the next.
- Discuss new insights and questions the map presents about each person in the group.

WORD OF ENCOURAGEMENT FROM ALLI

Leader, read this aloud or select a volunteer to read to the group.

When I was visiting Israel for the first time, I found myself completely disoriented a few days into my trip. Our group moved quickly between historical biblical sites, often traveling into the lives of people who lived a thousand years apart in time but only a few miles apart in Israel. I had to work very hard to keep it all straight, especially on one particular day when our sites ranged from something during Joshua's life in Gilgal, to a post-resurrection encounter with Jesus on the road to Emmaus, and finally to the place of an encounter between Samson and the Philistines. Without a map or a timeline, I was almost dizzy trying to keep up with the movements of time, geography, and biblical characters. I so badly needed some tools of ORIENTATION to help me. The Bible is a collection of sixty-six books by thirty-five(ish) authors, written over approximately 1,500 years. It's normal to need time and help to learn and clarify everything that is taking place. When I planned a second trip to Israel, I created a timeline for my group with all the people and places we were going to see. I didn't want them to feel quite as disoriented as I had!

We often tolerate a sense of confusion when we read the Bible, because it's a story that is consistent but told in pieces and parts that are not arranged chronologically or thematically. The practice of ORIENTATION is simply answering three basic questions: *Who? Where? When?* The Bible makes much more sense when you take the time to put the basics in place. It is not a theological textbook but a story and history of real people and places over time. Even better than untangling events, you'll find sweet places in God's heart that are visible only with seemingly academic tools like maps and timelines. If you get and keep your bearings through the practice of ORIENTATION, the Spirit can lead you to all kinds of new places!

NOW IT'S TIME TO TURN ON THE SESSION 3 VIDEO.

WATCH SESSION 3 VIDEO

Leader, stream the video or play the DVD.

ORIENTATION PRACTICE NOTES

Capture anything you want to remember about this practice as you watch the video. These notes will help you when practicing ORIENTATION as a group and on your own.

ORIENTATION

WHO are all the participants in this passage?

- Do you need another resource to understand WHO they truly are?

WHERE are the locations mentioned in the passage?

- Do you need another resource to understand WHERE this is taking place?

- What does the Spirit illuminate when you see where the story is taking place on a map?

WHEN is the story you are reading taking place?

- Would it help you to have a specific date or to understand it relative to something else? Or both?

- Do you need another resource to understand WHEN that is?

- What does the Spirit illuminate to you when you find the story you are reading on a biblical eras timeline?

(10 MINUTES)

DURING-VIDEO GROUP PRACTICE

Leader, invite the Holy Spirit into your practice time, read the passage and prompts aloud, and encourage your group to fill in the boxes. Briefly share your findings before you return to the video.

Jonah 1:1–10

The word of the LORD came to Jonah son of Amittai: "Go to the great city of Nineveh and preach against it, because its wickedness has come up before me."

But Jonah ran away from the LORD and headed for Tarshish. He went down to Joppa, where he found a ship bound for that port. After paying the fare, he went aboard and sailed for Tarshish to flee from the LORD.

Then the LORD sent a great wind on the sea, and such a violent storm arose that the ship threatened to break up. All the sailors were afraid and each cried out to his own god. And they threw the cargo into the sea to lighten the ship.

But Jonah had gone below deck, where he lay down and fell into a deep sleep. The captain went to him and said, "How can you sleep? Get up and call on your god! Maybe he will take notice of us so that we will not perish."

Then the sailors said to each other, "Come, let us cast lots to find out who is responsible for this calamity." They cast lots and the lot fell on Jonah. So they asked him, "Tell us, who is responsible for making all this trouble for us? What kind of work do you do? Where do you come from? What is your country? From what people are you?"

He answered, "I am a Hebrew and I worship the LORD, the God of heaven, who made the sea and the dry land."

This terrified them and they asked, "What have you done?" (They knew he was running away from the LORD, because he had already told them so.)

- WHO are all the participants in this passage?

- WHERE are the locations mentioned in the passage? (See Appendix A for help.)

- WHEN is the story of Jonah taking place?

TIME'S UP!

Return now to the video for a short wrap-up of this practice from Alli.

GROUP DISCUSSION

Leader, read each prompt to the group for deeper discussion. Do not be concerned if you don't make it through every question. Trust the Spirit to lead your discussion as your group needs, so that you can connect and grow.

1. Briefly share one experience where a lack of ORIENTATION frustrated you or prevented you from fully understanding something you read in the Bible.

2. Do you ever use extra materials (maps, timelines, or other aids) for ORIENTATION as you read or study the Bible? Have you found them helpful?

3. What was the most interesting thing you learned about the story of Jonah as you practiced ORIENTATION and LISTENED to Alli's group?

4. What about this practice intrigued you most and why? What challenged you and why?

5. Alli quoted one of her seminary professors who said, "The worst thing about reading the Bible is that all the parts assume you know every other part." What is one part of the Bible story you have questions about? After thinking about the practice of ORIENTATION, what might help you understand that part better?

6. Discuss how good overall ORIENTATION inside the Bible leads you to understand more than the words you are reading.

7. Of the three practices we have learned in *Spirit-Led Bible Study* so far, which practice is the most challenging or most exciting, and which have you already been practicing? OBSERVATION/LISTENING/ORIENTATION

8. In our group practice, how did ORIENTATION to Jonah 1:1–10 sharpen, deepen, or change your understanding of . . .

- God?
- Yourself or humanity?
- Living a life of faith?

PREP FOR INDIVIDUAL STUDY

Leader, read this to the group.

This week you will read multiple passages of Scripture on your own and practice ORIENTATION. On the following pages, you will find handy reference charts for how to practice ORIENTATION well. I encourage you to dive into this practice with your whole heart and ask the Holy Spirit to reveal something new and edifying to you as you do!

CLOSING PRAYER

Leader, read this prayer over your group before dismissing.

Lord, thank You for Your commitment to showing us who You are even through maps and timelines. Give us the curiosity and endurance to get and stay ORIENTED to Your Word. In Jesus' name,

Amen

HOW-TO PRACTICE: ORIENTATION

The following pages are simple key resources to use as your general guide. Each page (and book of the Bible) corresponds to an era or movement along this Biblical Eras timeline.

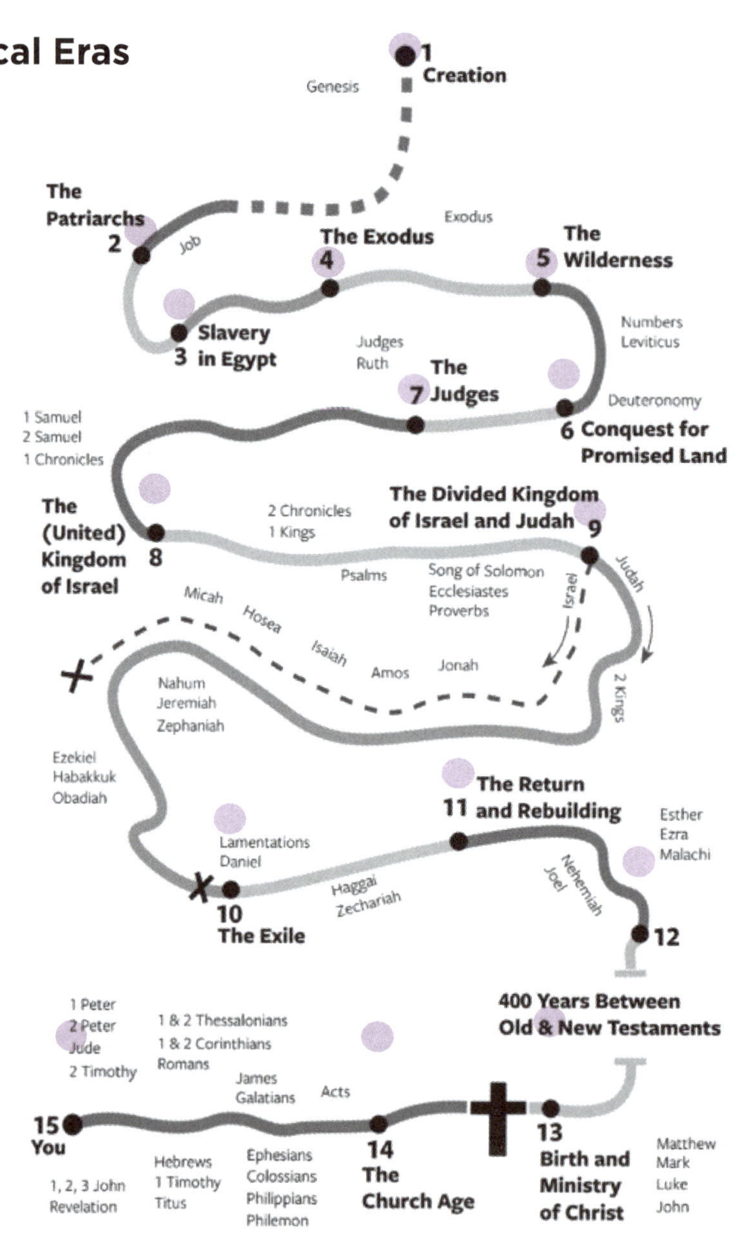

The Patriarchs to Jesus

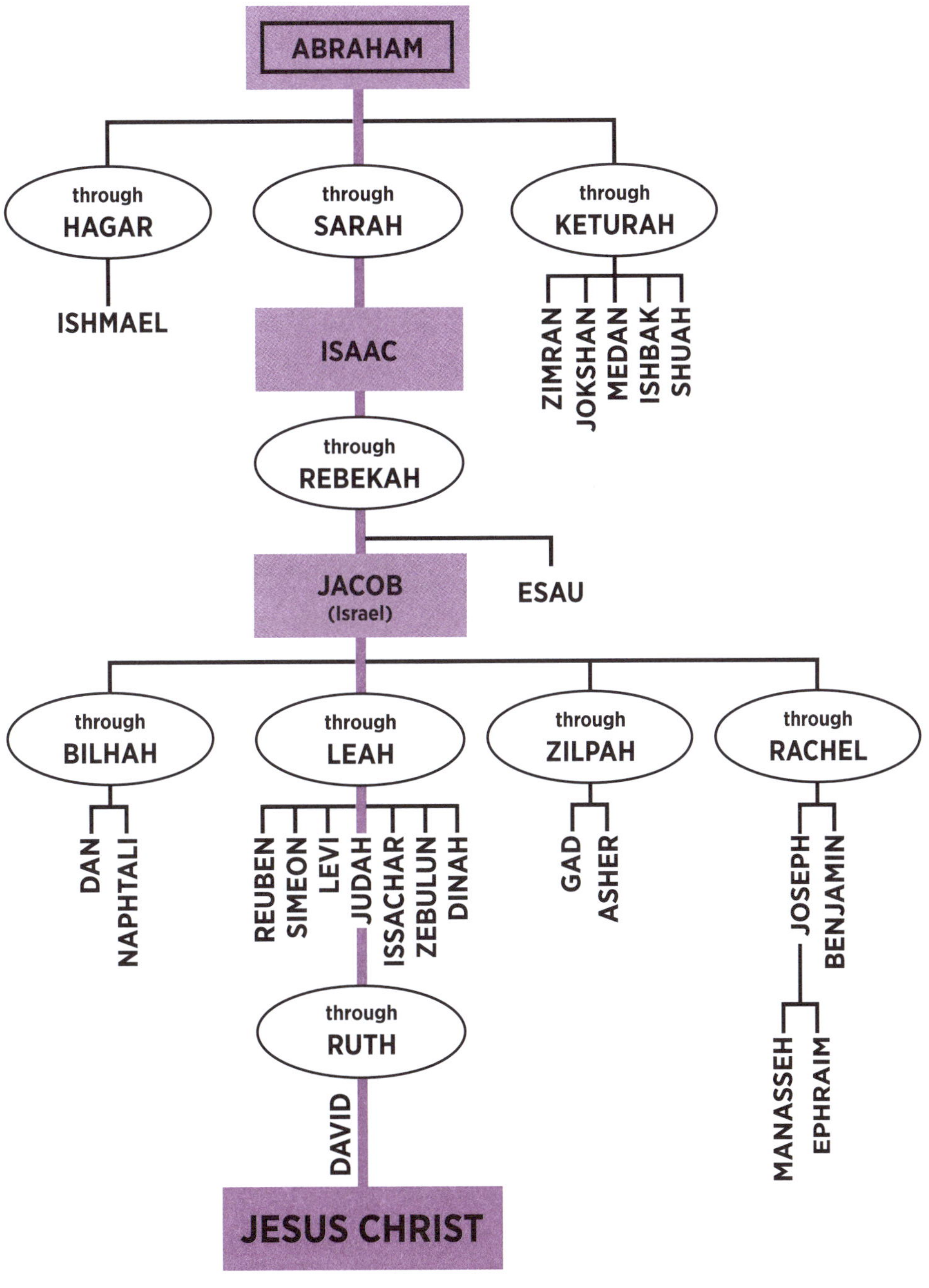

The Exodus & Wilderness

Conquest for Promised Land: Twelve Tribes of Israel

The Prophets During Kingdoms

PROHPET*	NAME MEANS	PLACE OF ACTIVITY	APPROXIMATE TIME PERIOD**	SCRIPTURE***
ISAIAH	"Yahweh is salvation"	Judah	739-685 BC	Isaiah 1:1; 6:1; 7:1; 20:1; 36–39; Hebrews 11:37
JEREMIAH	"Yahweh exalts"	Judah	627-580 BC	Jeremiah 1:2–3; 3:6; 11:21–23; 21:1; 22:11; 24:1; 25:1–3, 8–12; 26:1; 27:1; 37–40; 52:31–33
EZEKIEL	"Yahweh strengthens"	Babylon	592-570 BC	Ezra 1:1–3; 24:1–2; 33:21
DANIEL	"Yahweh is my judge"	Babylon Persia	606-530 BC	Daniel 1:1–7; 1–4; 5:1ff; 6:1ff; 10:1
HOSEA	"salvation"	Israel	760-720 BC	Hosea 1:1
JOEL	"Yahweh is God"	Judah	830 BC? (if ministry at an early date)	(locust and Day of the Lord pictures in Joel)
AMOS	"burden bearer"	Israel	760 BC	Amos 1:1; 7:12–17; 9:11–12
OBADIAH	"servant of Yahweh"	Judah?	845 BC?	(Obadiah 1–9 quoted in Jeremiah 49:7–16) (2 Kings 8:20)
JONAH	"dove"	Israel (Nineveh)	780-760 BC	2 Kings 14:25; Jonah 1:1; 3:1
MICAH	"Who is like Yahweh?"	Judah	737-690 BC	Micah 1:1
NAHUM	"comfort/ consolation"	Judah	after 664 BC before 612 BC	Nahum 1:1 (Fall of Nineveh)
HABAKKUK	"embracer"	Judah	620-610 BC?	Habakkuk 1:6 (Babylon)
ZEPHANIAH	"Yahweh hides/ treasures/protects"	Judah	640-608 BC	Zephaniah 1:1
HAGGAI	"my feast/festival"	Judah (post-exile)	520-516 BC	Haggai 1:1; 2:10; 2:20; Ezra 5–6
ZECHARIAH	"Yahweh remembers"	Judah (post-exile)	520-518 BC	Zechariah 1:1; 7:1; Haggai 1:1
MALACHI	"my messenger/ angel"	Judah (post-exile)	430 BC	Malachi 1:7, 8, 10; 3:1

Divided Kingdoms: Israel and Judah

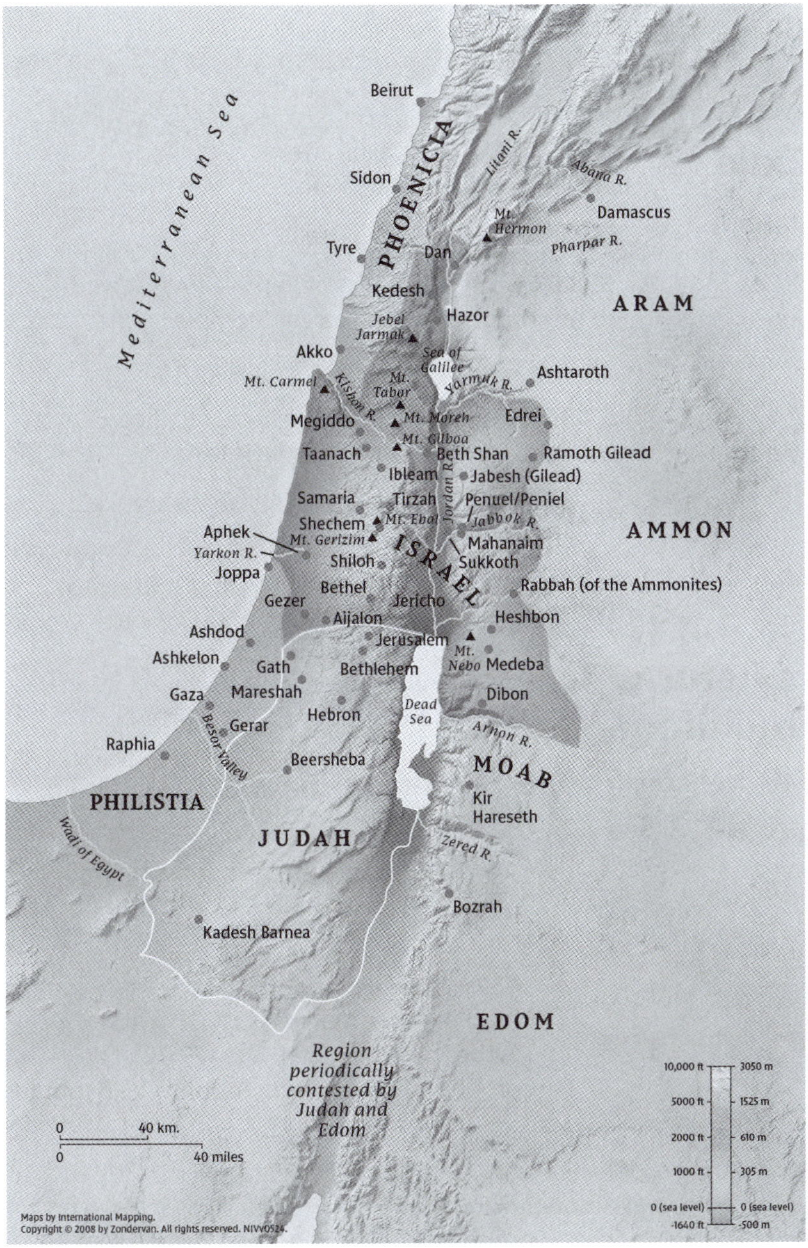

Maps by International Mapping.
Copyright © 2008 by Zondervan. All rights reserved. NIVV0524.

Exile Through Return

10
The Exile

Lamentations
Daniel

605-535 BC 70 year exile after Babylon conquers Jerusalem.

539 BC Babylon falls to Persia.

538 BC Decree by Cyrus of Persia allows Jews to return to Jerusalem, rebuild temple.

538-537 BC First wave of exiles return.

Haggai
Zechariah

536 BC Altar of temple finished, sacrifices begin. Foundation of temple is laid.

536-520 BC Samaritan, Persian resistance ended rebuilding for 16 years.

520 BC Haggai and Zechariah prophesy to the people about rebuilding the temple.

11
The Return and Rebuilding

Nehemiah
Joel

Esther
Ezra
Malachi

483-473 BC Book of Esther written.

457-458 BC Second wave of exiles return.

444 BC Third wave of exiles return.

432-425 BC Possible date for prophecies of Malachi, last OT writing. (Other possible date: 480-470 BC). No prophets from Malachi to John the Baptist.

12
400 Years

331 BC Close of OT. Alexander the Great defeats Persia Israel under Hellenistic, Hasmonean and then Roman rule. Rome in power as NT begins.

(See page 82 for the full Biblical Timeline.)

Israel and Judah's Exiles

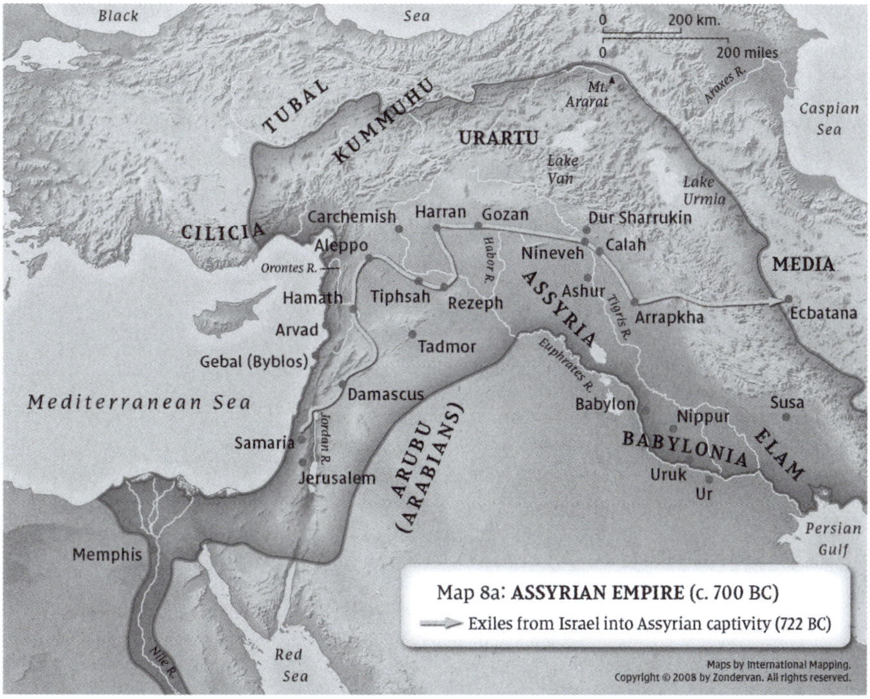

Map 8a: **ASSYRIAN EMPIRE** (c. 700 BC)

Exiles from Israel into Assyrian captivity (722 BC)

Maps by International Mapping.
Copyright © 2008 by Zondervan. All rights reserved.

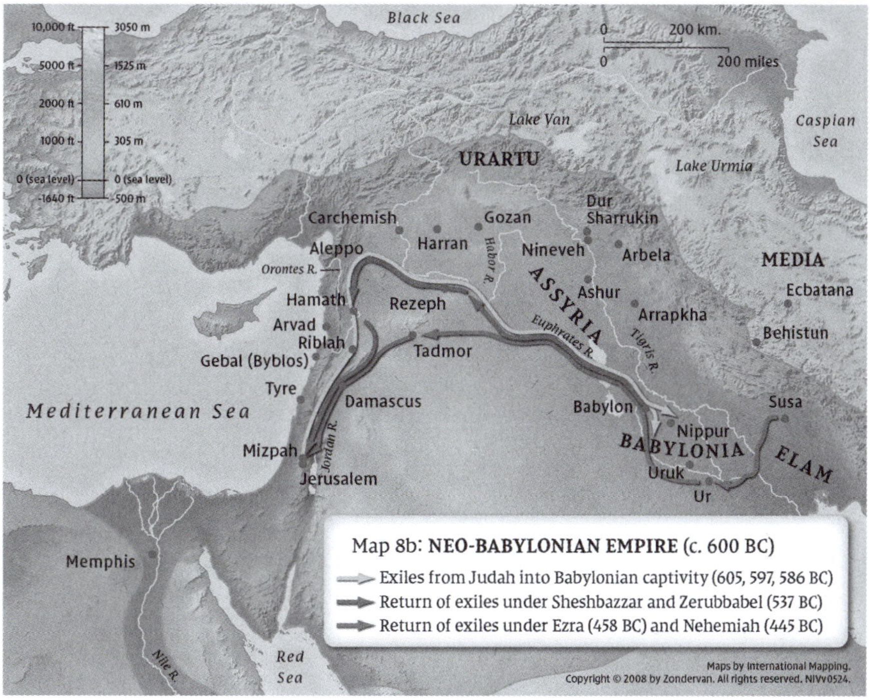

Map 8b: **NEO-BABYLONIAN EMPIRE** (c. 600 BC)

Exiles from Judah into Babylonian captivity (605, 597, 586 BC)

Return of exiles under Sheshbazzar and Zerubbabel (537 BC)

Return of exiles under Ezra (458 BC) and Nehemiah (445 BC)

Maps by International Mapping.
Copyright © 2008 by Zondervan. All rights reserved. NIVv0524.

Jesus' Birth and Early Life

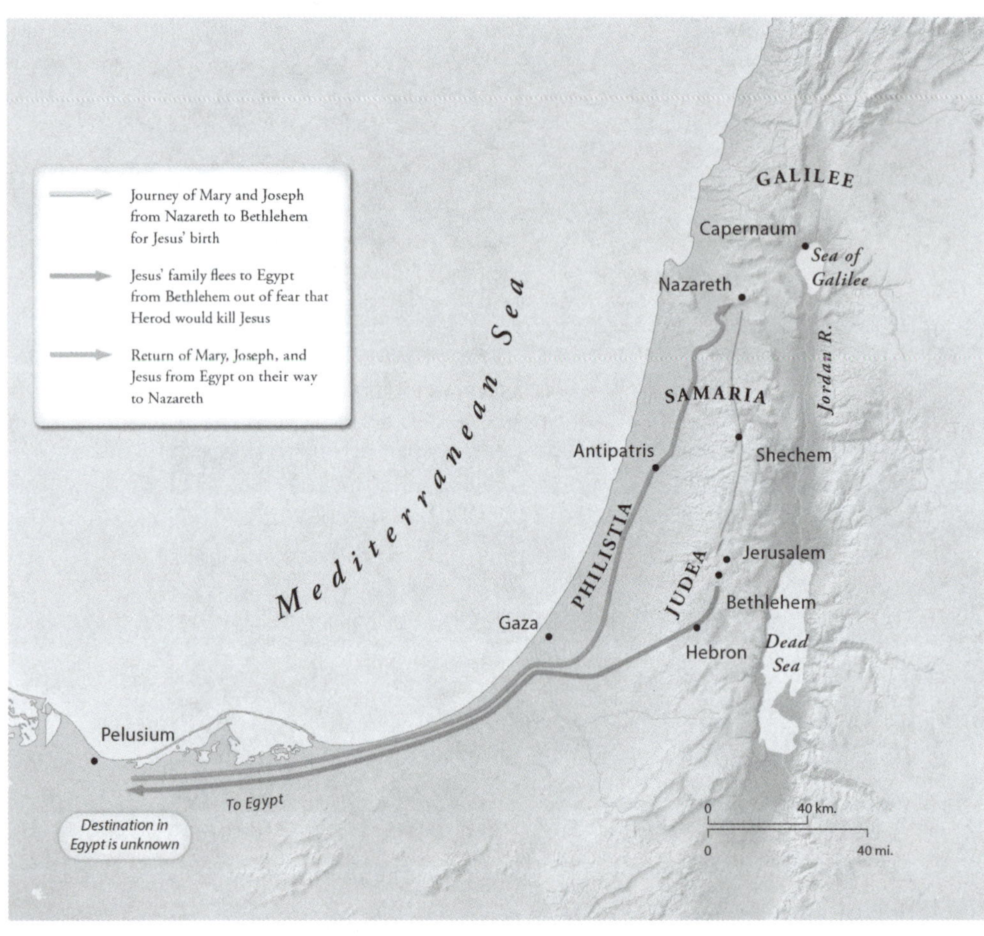

Early Church: Paul's Missionary Journeys

SESSION 3

ORIENTATION

INDIVIDUAL PRACTICE

Today, you are diving headfirst into ORIENTATION on your own!
For some of you, this could be the most exciting day of this study so far. For others, this might feel overwhelming, and for yet others, you may already be down one of many rabbit holes exploring the details and connections in the biblical narrative. Remember, every time you open and engage your Bible you are engaging with God. Through His Spirit, you are learning, and new things are being revealed. Trust this process. Trust God in it. Trust that the Holy Spirit will not leave you confused or wondering longer than necessary. Trust that sometimes your questions are exactly where the Spirit meets you with the most answers!

ORIENTATION PRACTICE Day 1

Spend a few minutes in prayer now, asking the Holy Spirit to be your guide as you read the Scriptures and to give insight, understanding, and connections as you go.

- Read the Scripture passage.
- Use the maps and resources found on the HOW-TO PRACTICE: ORIENTATION, pages 82–91.
- Answer the three questions of WHO, WHERE, and WHEN to practice getting ORIENTED.

Haggai 1:1–11

In the second year of King Darius, on the first day of the sixth month, the word of the LORD came through the prophet Haggai to Zerubbabel son of Shealtiel, governor of Judah, and to Joshua son of Jozadak, the high priest:

This is what the LORD Almighty says: "These people say, 'The time has not yet come to rebuild the LORD's house.'"

Then the word of the LORD came through the prophet Haggai: "Is it a time for you yourselves to be living in your paneled houses, while this house remains a ruin?"

Now this is what the LORD Almighty says: "Give careful thought to your ways. You have planted much, but harvested little. You eat, but never have enough. You drink, but never have your fill. You put on clothes, but are not warm. You earn wages, only to put them in a purse with holes in it."

This is what the LORD Almighty says: "Give careful thought to your ways. Go up into the mountains and bring down timber and build my house, so that I may take pleasure in it and be honored," says the LORD. "You expected much, but see, it turned out to be little. What you brought home, I blew away. Why?" declares the LORD Almighty. "Because of my house, which remains a ruin, while each of you is busy with your own house. Therefore, because of you the heavens have withheld their dew and the earth its crops. I called for a drought on the fields and the mountains, on the grain, the new wine, the olive oil and everything else the ground produces, on people and livestock, and on all the labor of your hands."

WHO are all the participants in this passage?

- Write down any/all names mentioned and any details given about who they are.

- What questions do you have? What are you curious about?

- Is there a nudge from the Spirit to find out anything more about WHO?

- Do you need another resource to understand WHO they truly are? If so, go find it! Write down whatever you learn to share with your group.

WHERE are the locations mentioned in the passage?

- Write down any/all places mentioned.

- What questions do you have? What are you curious about?

- Is there a nudge from the Spirit to find out anything more about WHERE?

- Do you need another resource to understand WHERE this is taking place? (See pages 82–86.)

- What does the Spirit illuminate when you see where Haggai is on a map?

WHEN is the story of Haggai taking place?

- Write down any information about when this is taking place.

- What questions do you have? What are you curious about?

- Is there a nudge from the Spirit to find out anything more about WHEN?

- Would it help you to have a specific date or to understand it relative to something else? Or both?

- Do you need another resource to understand WHEN this is? Where might you find it? If you find it, record it here so you can share and return to it in future Bible study ORIENTATION practice.

- What does the Spirit illuminate to you when you find Haggai on the Biblical Eras timeline (page 82)?

How did better ORIENTATION to Haggai 1:1–11 (understanding who/where/when) sharpen, deepen, or change your understanding of . . .

- God?
- Yourself or humanity?
- Living a life of faith?

ORIENTATION PRACTICE Day 2

Spend a few minutes in prayer now, asking the Holy Spirit to be your guide as you read the Scriptures and to give insight, understanding, and connections as you go.

- Read the Scripture passage.
- Use the maps and resources found on the HOW-TO PRACTICE: ORIENTATION, pages 82–91.
- Answer the three questions of WHO, WHERE, and WHEN to practice getting ORIENTED.

2 Samuel 7:1–17

After the king was settled in his palace and the LORD had given him rest from all his enemies around him, he said to Nathan the prophet, "Here I am, living in a house of cedar, while the ark of God remains in a tent."

Nathan replied to the king, "Whatever you have in mind, go ahead and do it, for the LORD is with you."

But that night the word of the LORD came to Nathan, saying:

"Go and tell my servant David, 'This is what the LORD says: Are you the one to build me a house to dwell in? I have not dwelt in a house from the day I brought the Israelites up out of Egypt to this day. I have been moving from place to place with a tent as my dwelling. Wherever I have moved with all the Israelites, did I ever say to any of their rulers whom I commanded to shepherd my people Israel, "Why have you not built me a house of cedar?"'

"Now then, tell my servant David, 'This is what the LORD Almighty says: I took you from the pasture, from tending the flock, and appointed you ruler over my people Israel. I have been with you wherever you have gone, and I have cut off all your enemies from before you. Now I will make your name great, like the names of the greatest men on earth. And I will provide a place for my people Israel and will plant them so that they can have a home of their own and no longer be disturbed. Wicked people will not oppress them anymore, as they did at the beginning and have done ever since the time I appointed leaders over my people Israel. I will also give you rest from all your enemies.

"'The LORD declares to you that the LORD himself will establish a house for you: When your days are over and you rest with your ancestors, I will raise up your offspring to succeed you, your own flesh and blood, and I will establish his kingdom. He is the one who will build a house for my Name, and I will establish the throne of his kingdom forever. I will be his father, and he will be my son. When he does wrong, I will punish him with a rod wielded by men, with floggings inflicted by human hands. But my love will never be taken away from him, as I took it away from Saul, whom I removed from before you. Your house and your kingdom will endure forever before me; your throne will be established forever.'"

Nathan reported to David all the words of this entire revelation.

WHO are all the participants in this passage?

- Write down any/all names mentioned and any details given about who they are.

- What questions do you have? What are you curious about?

- Is there a nudge from the Spirit to find out anything more about WHO?

- Do you need another resource to understand WHO they truly are?

- If so, go find it! Write down whatever you learn to share with your group.

WHERE are the locations mentioned in the passage?

- Write down any/all places mentioned.

- What questions do you have? What are you curious about?

- Is there a nudge from the Spirit to find out anything more about WHERE?

- Do you need another resource to understand WHERE this is taking place? (See pages 82–86.)

- What does the Spirit illuminate when you see where this is taking place on a map?

WHEN is the story of 2 Samuel taking place?

- Write down any information about when this is taking place.

- What questions do you have? What are you curious about?

- Is there a nudge from the Spirit to find out anything more about WHEN?

- Would it help you to have a specific date or to understand it relative to something else? Or both?

- Do you need another resource to understand WHEN this is? Where might you find it? If you find it, record it here so you can share and return to it in future Bible study ORIENTATION practice.

- What does the Spirit illuminate to you when you find 2 Samuel on the Biblical Eras Timeline (page 82)?

How did better ORIENTATION to 2 Samuel 7:1–17 (understanding who/where/when) sharpen, deepen, or change your understanding of . . .

- God?

- Yourself or humanity?

- Living a life of faith?

ORIENTATION PRACTICE Day 3

Spend a few minutes in prayer now, asking the Holy Spirit to be your guide as you read the Scriptures and to give insight, understanding, and connections as you go.

- Read the Scripture passage.
- Use the maps and resources found on the HOW-TO PRACTICE: ORIENTATION, pages 82–91.
- Answer the three questions of WHO, WHERE, and WHEN to practice getting ORIENTED.

Mark 1:1–5

The beginning of the good news about Jesus the Messiah, the Son of God, as it is written in Isaiah the prophet:

"I will send my messenger ahead of you,
who will prepare your way"—
"a voice of one calling in the wilderness,
'Prepare the way for the Lord,
make straight paths for him.'"

And so John the Baptist appeared in the wilderness, preaching a baptism of repentance for the forgiveness of sins. The whole Judean countryside and all the people of Jerusalem went out to him. Confessing their sins, they were baptized by him in the Jordan River.

WHO are all the participants in this passage?

- Write down any/all names mentioned and any details given about who they are.

- What questions do you have? What are you curious about?

- Is there a nudge from the Spirit to find out anything more about WHO?

- Do you need another resource to understand WHO they truly are?

- If so, go find it! Write down whatever you learn to share with your group.

WHERE are the locations mentioned in the passage?

- Write down any/all places mentioned.

- What questions do you have? What are you curious about?

- Is there a nudge from the Spirit to find out anything more about WHERE?

- Do you need another resource to understand WHERE this is taking place? (See pages 82–86.)

- What does the Spirit illuminate when you see where this is taking place on a map?

WHEN is the story of Mark's gospel taking place?

- Write down any information about when this is taking place.

- What questions do you have? What are you curious about?

- Is there a nudge from the Spirit to find out anything more about WHEN?

- Would it help you to have a specific date or to understand it relative to something else? Or both?

- Do you need another resource to understand WHEN this is? Where might you find it? If you find it, record it here so you can share and return to it in future Bible study ORIENTATION practice.

- What does the Spirit illuminate to you when you find Mark on the Biblical Eras Timeline (page 82)?

How did better ORIENTATION to Mark 1:1–5 (understanding who/where/when) sharpen, deepen, or change your understanding of . . .

- God?

- Yourself or humanity?

- Living a life of faith?

Staying ORIENTED is worth the time and effort so you don't get lost in the pages of the Bible. Good work. Keep going!

SESSION 4

PRAYER

GROUP MEETING

Leader, read this aloud to the group.

Welcome to *Spirit-Led Bible Study* Session 4!

This week is all about PRAYER. In this session, you will LISTEN to the Holy Spirit to create PRAYERS using words straight from the Bible! PRAYING through the Scriptures is a powerful and potent practice that is also surprisingly personal. Most people tend to PRAY with their own priorities and people in mind, but you can seek out *what is important to God*. If you do, it will be a better conversation every time.

PRAYING Scripture becomes a participation in the will that God has already expressed through the Spirit.

In the Bible, God's Living Word, we can hear God speaking to us and we respond in prayer, though we should not call this simply a "response." Through the Word and Spirit, prayer becomes answering God—a full conversation.

Timothy Keller, *Prayer*

REVIEW SESSION 3 INDIVIDUAL PRACTICE

Leader, read these instructions aloud to the group before you begin. I recommend setting a timer so you don't spend too much time here. You'll need most of your group time for the new practice of PRAYER.

For homework, you spent time getting oriented to the book of Haggai. That little book fills in big details from a lesser-known part of Scripture. The beauty of studying Scripture with others is how the Spirit is alive and active in all of us differently, so take the time now to discuss as a group.

Share the curiosities you had (or nudges from the Holy Spirit!) about the ORIENTATION questions of who, where, and when from Haggai 1:1–11.

What did you learn as you investigated the answers? What tools did you use to investigate?

Did anyone go beyond the resources provided and investigate something else? If so, share it!

What value did you take away from the practice of ORIENTATION?

Will you keep practicing ORIENTATION as you read the Bible?
Why or why not?

In what ways did better ORIENTATION to Haggai 1:1–11 (understanding who/where/when) sharpen, deepen, or change your understanding of . . .

- God?
- Yourself or humanity?
- Living a life of faith?

Now it's time to begin our next *Spirit-Led Bible Study* practice!

WARM-UP

Leader, read these instructions aloud to the group before the timer begins.

Share with your group the **top three priorities** you have in your life for the next one to two weeks. Someone make a list as these are shared.

Discuss the themes or similarities in the priorities that were shared. Then, someone pray for these on behalf of the group.

WORD OF ENCOURAGEMENT FROM ALLI

Leader, read this aloud or select a volunteer to read to the group.

Like most people, I occasionally wonder if my PRAYERS really matter, if God is LISTENING every time I talk to Him, and if I'm even doing it "right." I have come to understand that the answer to all three of those questions is yes. I believe every word you speak to God is precious and valuable to Him. Still, deeper knowledge and understanding of God changes the conversation. Going deeper into the Bible will begin to shift the topics and ways you speak to God. You will become more aligned with His heart. The practice of PRAYING from Scripture is my personal favorite way to PRAY.

This kind of PRAYER puts God in His proper place—as the Alpha and the Omega, and sovereign over everything in between. Rather than let your own thoughts or whims form the basis of conversation with God, you can let the Spirit direct the priorities of your PRAYERS. When I use this practice, I gain a sense of confidence knowing my words definitely reflect God's will. You are about to join God's life and plans, instead of asking Him to join yours. Instead of advocating for what you want in your day, week, family, and work, you will advocate for God's priorities in those places. And yet, I have never finished this style of PRAYER and thought, *I didn't get to talk to God about what matters to me*. Instead, when I use this practice, I feel like my whole life shifts toward what matters to Him.

NOW IT'S TIME TO TURN ON THE SESSION 4 VIDEO.

WATCH SESSION 4 VIDEO

Leader, stream the video or play the DVD.

PRAYER PRACTICE NOTES

Capture anything you want to remember about this practice as you watch the video. These notes will help you when you PRAY as a group and on your own.

FIVE TYPES OF PRAYER

- **Praise.** Dwell on God and all His amazing attributes in the worship of praise! (Psalm 145)
- **Thank**. PRAY with gratitude for whatever is revealed in your passage that acknowledges God as sovereign, good, and worthy, remembering how He has acted in the past. (1 Thessalonians 5:18)
- **Ask.** You can petition God for all sorts of things! When you use this type of PRAYER in Scripture stay focused on the priorities revealed in the passage. (James 1:5)
- **Confess.** This sets us free and makes our PRAYERS powerful and unhindered. Whenever a passage elicits personal confession, approach God in confidence that you will find His mercy in Christ. (Psalm 51)
- **Fight.** In Christ you have authority to do battle with the forces of evil, break strongholds, and request the life promised to you by God. You have the power and privilege to PRAY "on earth as it is in heaven" (Matthew 6:10). (2 Corinthians 10:4–5)

In Appendix B you will find a list of common biblical verbs to help you in creating PRAYERS if you need them.

(10 MINUTES)

DURING-VIDEO GROUP PRACTICE

Leader, invite the Holy Spirit into your practice time, read the passage and prompts aloud, and encourage your group to fill in the boxes. Briefly share your findings before you return to the video.

Daniel 6:16–23

So the king gave the order, and they brought Daniel and threw him into the lions' den. The king said to Daniel, "May your God, whom you serve continually, rescue you!"

A stone was brought and placed over the mouth of the den, and the king sealed it with his own signet ring and with the rings of his nobles, so that Daniel's situation might not be changed. Then the king returned to his palace and spent the night without eating and without any entertainment being brought to him. And he could not sleep.

At the first light of dawn, the king got up and hurried to the lions' den. When he came near the den, he called to Daniel in an anguished voice, "Daniel, servant of the living God, has your God, whom you serve continually, been able to rescue you from the lions?"

Daniel answered, "May the king live forever! My God sent his angel, and he shut the mouths of the lions. They have not hurt me, because I was found innocent in his sight. Nor have I ever done any wrong before you, Your Majesty."

The king was overjoyed and gave orders to lift Daniel out of the den. And when Daniel was lifted from the den, no wound was found on him, because he had trusted in his God.

What is important to God in this passage?

MY PRACTICE PRAYER

PRAISE / THANK / ASK / CONFESS / FIGHT

TIME'S UP!

Return now to the video for a short wrap-up of this practice from Alli.

GROUP DISCUSSION

Leader, read each prompt to the group for deeper discussion. Do not be concerned if you don't make it through every question. Trust the Spirit to lead your discussion as your group needs, so that you can connect and grow.

1. Have you ever practiced PRAYER starting with the words of Scripture instead of starting with your personal needs or concerns?

2. If PRAYER is ever a challenge for you, what is something you learned today that encourages you or gives you confidence to try PRAYER as a practice of Bible study?

3. Which type of PRAYER intrigued you most and why? Which challenges you and why?

4. Alli noted that often when you read Scripture, your own concerns come to mind, but so do those far beyond you: "PRAYING the Word of God is a way the Spirit works to impact the world around you every day." Share a time you practiced PRAYER on behalf of other people or circumstances that would have no direct effect on you.

5. Describe something you learned from the passage in Daniel and how it impacts your understanding of PRAYER. What was it that kept Daniel safe in the lions' den? Have you experienced PRAYER in this same way? Share.

6. What challenges or barriers might you have in aligning your PRAYERS with the priorities, plans, or personality of God? Talk as a group about how you can overcome these barriers.

7. In our group practice, how did writing your PRAYER using Daniel 6:16–23 sharpen, deepen, or change your understanding of . . .

   - God?
   - Yourself or humanity?
   - Living a life of faith?

PREP FOR INDIVIDUAL STUDY

Leader, read this to the group.

This week you will read multiple passages of Scripture on your own and practice PRAYER. On the following pages, you will find a handy reference chart for how to practice PRAYER well. I encourage you to dive into this practice with your whole heart and ask the Holy Spirit to reveal something new and edifying to you as you do!

CLOSING PRAYER

Leader, read this prayer over your group before dismissing.

Lord, teach us to PRAY according to Your heart. We want Your will—not ours—to be done today and in our lives. Encourage us with glimpses of what impact we can have when we partner with You in PRAYER to bring heaven down to earth, right here and now. In Jesus' name,

Amen

FIVE TYPES OF PRAYER

PRAISE | Psalm 145

Dwell on God and all His amazing attributes in the worship of praise!

THANK | 1 Thessalonians 5:18

PRAY with gratitude for whatever is revealed in your passage that acknowledges God as sovereign, good, and worthy, remembering how He has acted in the past.

ASK | James 1:5

You can petition God for all sorts of things! When you use this type of PRAYER in Scripture, stay focused on the priorities revealed in the passage.

CONFESS | Psalm 51

This sets us free and makes our PRAYERS powerful and unhindered. Whenever a passage elicits personal confession, approach God in confidence that you will find His mercy in Christ.

FIGHT | 2 Corinthians 10:4–5

In Christ you have authority to do battle with the forces of evil, break strongholds, and request the life promised to you by God. You have the power and privilege to PRAY "on earth as it is in heaven" (Matthew 6:10).

QUESTIONS TO ASK AS YOU PRAY A PASSAGE

What new discovery/discoveries are in the text?
(Hint: These are going to come from making good OBSERVATIONS!)

What do I think is important to God as a result of reading this passage? What are His **plans, priorities, and personality/character** as revealed in the passage? (Hint: I like to look at verbs to get specific about what God is doing in the passage.)

What people and places come to mind to PRAY for as I read this passage? (Hint: names, schools, countries, leaders, families, companies, parts of the world or church)

What type of PRAYER does this make me think of PRAYING? (Hint: Praise, Thank, Ask, Confess, Fight)

What PRAYERS can I PRAY from this passage?

SESSION 4

PRAYER

INDIVIDUAL PRACTICE

This week you are going to try the practice of PRAYER on your own.

Just as you have learned in the other Bible study practices, PRAYER requires a true surrender and connection with the Holy Spirit through the Word. Take your time as you read the Scripture passages this week, and notice how reading Scripture using the other Bible study practices you've learned can enhance your ability to practice PRAYER in your study time.

PRAYER PRACTICE Day 1

Form PRAYERS from this passage of Scripture:

Acts 12:5–11

So Peter was kept in prison, but the church was earnestly praying to God for him.

The night before Herod was to bring him to trial, Peter was sleeping between two soldiers, bound with two chains, and sentries stood guard at the entrance. Suddenly an angel of the Lord appeared and a light shone in the cell. He struck Peter on the side and woke him up. "Quick, get up!" he said, and the chains fell off Peter's wrists.

Then the angel said to him, "Put on your clothes and sandals." And Peter did so. "Wrap your cloak around you and follow me," the angel told him. Peter followed him out of the prison, but he had no idea that what the angel was doing was really happening; he thought he was seeing a vision. They passed the first and second guards and came to the iron gate leading to the city. It opened for them by itself, and they went through it. When they had walked the length of one street, suddenly the angel left him.

Then Peter came to himself and said, "Now I know without a doubt that the Lord has sent his angel and rescued me from Herod's clutches and from everything the Jewish people were hoping would happen."

What new discovery/discoveries are in the text?
(Hint: These are going to come from making good OBSERVATIONS!)

What do I think is important to God as a result of reading this passage? What are His **plans, priorities, and personality/character** as revealed in the passage? *(Hint: I like to look at verbs to get specific about what God is doing in the passage.)*

What people and places come to mind to PRAY for as I read this passage? *(Hint: names, schools, countries, leaders, families, companies, parts of the world or church)*

What type of PRAYER does this make me think of PRAYING? *(Hint: Praise, Thank, Ask, Confess, Fight)*

What PRAYERS can I PRAY from this passage?

Take time now to PRAY the PRAYERS you just formed.

How did PRAYING through Acts 12:5–11 sharpen, deepen, or change your understanding of . . .

- God?
- Yourself or humanity?
- Living a life of faith?

PRAYER PRACTICE Day 2

Form PRAYERS from this passage of Scripture:

Ecclesiastes 12:9–14

Not only was the Teacher wise, but he also imparted knowledge to the people. He pondered and searched out and set in order many proverbs. The Teacher searched to find just the right words, and what he wrote was upright and true.

The words of the wise are like goads, their collected sayings like firmly embedded nails—given by one shepherd. Be warned, my son, of anything in addition to them.

Of making many books there is no end, and much study wearies the body.

Now all has been heard;
here is the conclusion of the matter:
Fear God and keep his commandments,
for this is the duty of all mankind.
For God will bring every deed into judgment,
including every hidden thing,
whether it is good or evil.

What new discovery/discoveries are in the text? *(Hint: These are going to come from making good OBSERVATIONS!)*

What do I think is important to God as a result of reading this passage? What are His **plans, priorities, and personality/character** as revealed in the passage? *(Hint: I like to look at verbs to get specific about what God is doing in the passage.)*

What people and places come to mind to PRAY for as I read this passage? *(Hint: names, schools, countries, leaders, families, companies, parts of the world or church)*

What type of PRAYER does this make me think of PRAYING? *(Hint: Praise, Thank, Ask, Confess, Fight)*

What PRAYERS can I PRAY from this passage?

Take time now to PRAY the PRAYERS you just formed.

How did PRAYING through Ecclesiastes 12:9–14 sharpen, deepen, or change your understanding of . . .

- God?
- Yourself or humanity?
- Living a life of faith?

PRAYER PRACTICE Day 3

Form PRAYERS from this passage of Scripture:

Revelation 21:1–4

Then I saw "a new heaven and a new earth," for the first heaven and the first earth had passed away, and there was no longer any sea. I saw the Holy City, the new Jerusalem, coming down out of heaven from God, prepared as a bride beautifully dressed for her husband. And I heard a loud voice from the throne saying, "Look! God's dwelling place is now among the people, and he will dwell with them. They will be his people, and God himself will be with them and be their God. 'He will wipe every tear from their eyes. There will be no more death' or mourning or crying or pain, for the old order of things has passed away."

What new discovery/discoveries are in the text? *(Hint: These are going to come from making good OBSERVATIONS!)*

What do I think is important to God as a result of reading this passage? What are His **plans, priorities, and personality/character** as revealed in the passage? *(Hint: I like to look at verbs to get specific about what God is doing in the passage.)*

What people and places come to mind to PRAY for as I read this passage? *(Hint: names, schools, countries, leaders, families, companies, parts of the world or church)*

What type of PRAYER does this make me think of PRAYING? *(Hint: Praise, Thank, Ask, Confess, Fight)*

What PRAYERS can I PRAY from this passage?

Take time now to PRAY the PRAYERS you just formed.

How did PRAYING through Revelation 21:1–4 sharpen, deepen, or change your understanding of . . .

- God?

- Yourself or humanity?

- Living a life of faith?

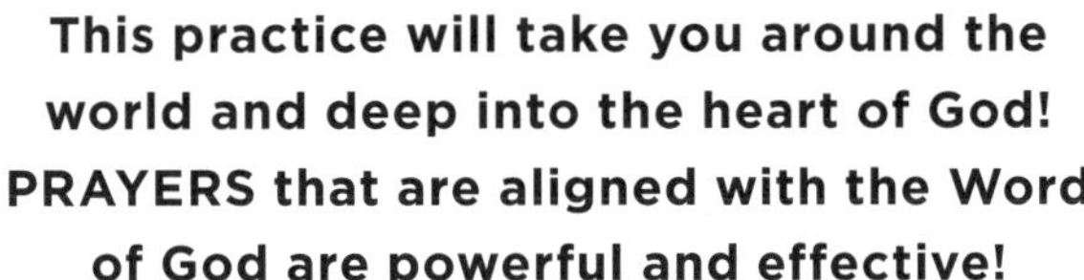

SESSION 5

CONTEXT

GROUP MEETING

Leader, read aloud to the group.

Welcome to *Spirit-Led Bible Study* Session 5!

Most people who approach the Bible to grow in their faith are hoping to find it chock-full of spiritual truth. And it is! But your desire for *spiritual truth* will often take you down rabbit trails in search of CONTEXT. The Holy Spirit reveals the wisdom of God as you read Scripture, so proper understanding of the stories, scenes, and situations in the Bible is critical. The often-repeated pithy saying that "context is king" is absolutely true. Missing CONTEXT often stands between you and the spiritual truth you come looking for in Scripture. So let's go learn how to find it.

The search for CONTEXT is actually the search for true meaning.

There is no such thing as the view from nowhere, or from everywhere for that matter.

Noam Shpancer, *The Good Psychologist*

REVIEW SESSION 4 INDIVIDUAL PRACTICE

Leader, read these instructions aloud to the group before you begin. I recommend setting a ten-minute timer so you don't spend too much time here. You'll need most of your group time for the new practice of CONTEXT.

You spent time on your own PRAYING on Day 1 Practice from Acts 12:5–11. One type of PRAYER that I PRAYED from this passage was praise that Jesus can set someone free from absolutely any situation!

First, take the time to share one answer per person for each of these questions:

- What do you think is important to God as a result of reading this passage?
- What similarities and differences do you notice in your group's answers?

Next, everyone:

- Share one PRAYER that you wrote down from this passage, and PRAY for these as a group (see Prayer Practice: Day 1 pages 123–125).
- Write down the PRAYER shared by the person on your left. Set yourself a reminder to PRAY for that every day this week.

In what ways did PRAYING through Acts 12:5–11 sharpen, deepen, or change your understanding of . . .

- God?
- Yourself or humanity?
- Living a life of faith?

Now it's time to begin our next *Spirit-Led Bible Study* practice!

WARM-UP

Leader, read these instructions aloud to the group before the timer begins.

The following quote was said by a historical person nearly everyone knows. Read it out loud and have everyone write down a potential explanation of WHAT this quote could be referring to and/or WHY it was said. (It's fine to guess the person, but your explanation of what and/or why is more important!)

"It is very beautiful over there."

Take turns sharing your explanations. After everyone has shared, read the real CONTEXT out loud.

These were the final words of Thomas Edison, believed to have been his brief glimpse of the afterlife just hours before he passed away in 1931.

CONTEXT is everything! Discuss the similarities and differences in your explanations and how they all compare to the real explanation. What did you learn about CONTEXT?

WORD OF ENCOURAGEMENT FROM ALLI

Leader, read this aloud or select a volunteer to read to the group.

One of my kids played me a little-known song by a well-known pop singer. It was hilariously inexplicable. She was singing about cows! I kept saying things like, "Why did she sing this song?" "Why does this even exist?" "What is this for? There must be a reason!" Her music had standard pop vibes, so I just couldn't fathom why this bizarre song was recorded. After my online investigation, I learned it was written in jest because of a costume she had to wear for a video shoot. After uncovering the CONTEXT, I could finally make sense of why she ever sang the song.

You can (and should!) do these kinds of investigations with Scripture. As you learn to ask and answer CONTEXT questions, the history, cultures, and theology at work in the background of the Bible not only alert you when something needs further explanation but also shed light on everything you read. I once asked, "Why are these odd details shared?" at the beginning of an Old Testament book—and they turned out to be CONTEXT from Jewish law, indicating a broken covenant with God. I would have missed the clear CONTEXT of the book if I hadn't stopped to investigate my question. Everything has CONTEXT. And CONTEXT reveals the true meaning of God's Word.

No one has perfect understanding, even after many years into Bible reading, so exploring CONTEXT is a lifelong, intentional endeavor. In this session, you will begin to hear and investigate the CONTEXT questions the Spirit stokes within you. If you find yourself asking what or why as you read the Bible, go find out! It's often a path the Spirit wants to lead you down for strengthening, encouragement, or comfort. Discovering the CONTEXT of the Bible is worth it every time!

NOW IT'S TIME TO TURN ON THE SESSION 5 VIDEO.

WATCH SESSION 5 VIDEO

Leader, stream the video or play the DVD.

CONTEXT PRACTICE NOTES

Capture anything you want to remember about this practice as you watch the video. These notes will help you when you practice as a group and on your own.

Meaning is determined by CONTEXT.

CONTEXT has many layers.

Every piece of Scripture sits inside these five CONTEXT frames:

- Frame 1—The Bible: What is the text immediately before and after this passage?
- Frame 2—What section of the book does it appear in?
- Frame 3—What book is it in?
- Frame 4—What connects this passage to the whole Bible?
- Frame 5—What connects this passage to the world outside the Bible? (culture, historical era, literary genre, geography, etc.)

Each frame illuminates answers to different what and why questions.

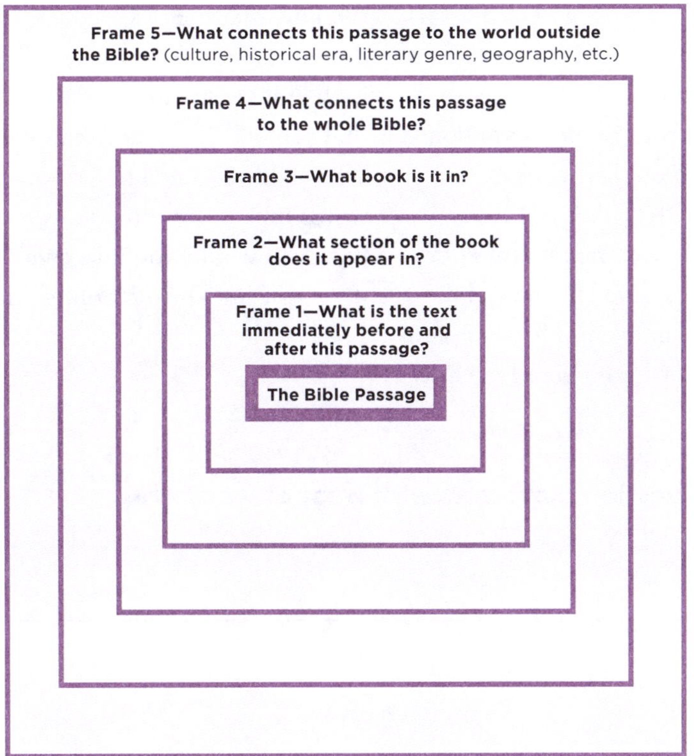

Leader, read this prayer aloud before reading the passage to the group:

Holy Spirit, open our minds to better understand Your Word. Father, thank You for giving us curiosity and the ability to seek You through learning. We want to know Your Word better so we can know and love You. In Jesus' name,

Amen

Matthew 12:1–8

At that time Jesus went through the grainfields on the Sabbath. His disciples were hungry and began to pick some heads of grain and eat them. When the Pharisees saw this, they said to him, "Look! Your disciples are doing what is unlawful on the Sabbath."

He answered, "Haven't you read what David did when he and his companions were hungry? He entered the house of God, and he and his companions ate the consecrated bread—which was not lawful for them to do, but only for the priests. Or haven't you read in the Law that the priests on Sabbath duty in the temple desecrate the Sabbath and yet are innocent? I tell you that something greater than the temple is here. If you had known what these words mean, 'I desire mercy, not sacrifice,' you would not have condemned the innocent. For the Son of Man is Lord of the Sabbath."

Write a single question that starts with *what* or *why* here.

Use the five frames to begin your search for CONTEXT. Which frame in the Learning Notes seems like it will help you answer the question you're asking?

CONTEXT FRAME I'M USING:

RESOURCES I NEED:

Explore the CONTEXT using that frame and make notes here:

What meaning was added to the passage from exploring its CONTEXT?

TIME'S UP!

Return now to the video for a short wrap-up of this practice from Alli.

GROUP DISCUSSION

Leader, read each prompt to the group for deeper discussion. Do not be concerned if you don't make it through every question. Trust the Spirit to lead your discussion as your group needs, so that you can connect and grow.

1. Share one way CONTEXT has mattered in your life. What impact does understanding context have on your relationships?

2. Talk about your experiences of reading or studying the Bible without full CONTEXT.

3. What might be the consequence of believing or responding to something without knowing the full CONTEXT? Why is this even more important when we are talking about, sharing, and responding to the Bible?

4. In what ways is CONTEXT different from ORIENTATION? In what ways is it the same?

5. How does thinking in frameworks help you discover CONTEXT? Consider this idea and discuss how you interact with others, strangers, and those foreign to your culture.

6. Alli noted that "the less familiar you are with something, the more you have to consciously seek the CONTEXT you need to get to the real meaning." What personal character traits might be important for seeking CONTEXT? Who in your group has some of these characteristics?

7. Discuss why pride works against your seeking CONTEXT. Share a time you didn't want to admit you lacked all the information or made a judgment without CONTEXT.

8. What practical obstacles do you face in seeking better CONTEXT as you read the Bible?

9. In our group practice, how did CONTEXT of Matthew 12:1–8 sharpen, deepen, or change your understanding of . . .

- God?
- Yourself or humanity?
- Living a life of faith?

PREP FOR INDIVIDUAL STUDY

Leader, read this to the group.

This week you will read multiple passages of Scripture on your own and practice CONTEXT. On the following pages, you will find a handy reference chart for how to practice CONTEXT well. I encourage you to dive into this practice with your whole heart and ask the Holy Spirit to reveal something new and edifying to you as you do!

CLOSING PRAYER

Leader, read this prayer over your group before dismissing.

Lord, please lead us to the CONTEXT we need to clearly understand You and Your Word. Help us pay attention to where You are leading and take us deeper. Please give us grace for the times we misunderstand You, and reveal Yourself more fully. In Jesus' name,

Amen

HOW-TO PRACTICE: CONTEXT

Meaning is determined by CONTEXT. CONTEXT has many layers. So you can add to your understanding of a passage by exploring up to five layers of CONTEXT. Every piece of Scripture sits inside these five CONTEXT frames. As you use each frame, your understanding of the CONTEXT grows, and meaning is added to what you are reading.

Each frame illuminates answers to different what and why questions you may ask as you read. You might need only one. You may need them all. Full meaning is found in all of these frames put together, but you can begin with the one that you think is likely to connect to the question you have. As you use any frame, ask yourself, *What meaning was added by this piece of CONTEXT?* Go in search of what you need to answer the question or curiosity the Spirit brought up within you.

	Frame 1	Frame 2	Frame 3	Frame 4	Frame 5
Resource You Might Need	Bible	Bible	Bible	Cross-Referene Tools	Study Bible Notes
	Study Bible Notes	Study Bible Notes	Study Bible Notes	Commentaries	Bible Background Commentaries
	Commentaries	Verse-by-Verse Commentaries	Book Introduction	Topical Bibles	Bible Dictionary & Encyclopedia
		Synthetic Outline or Structural Outline	Book Summary Chart		Historical & Cultural Studies
					Bible Atlas

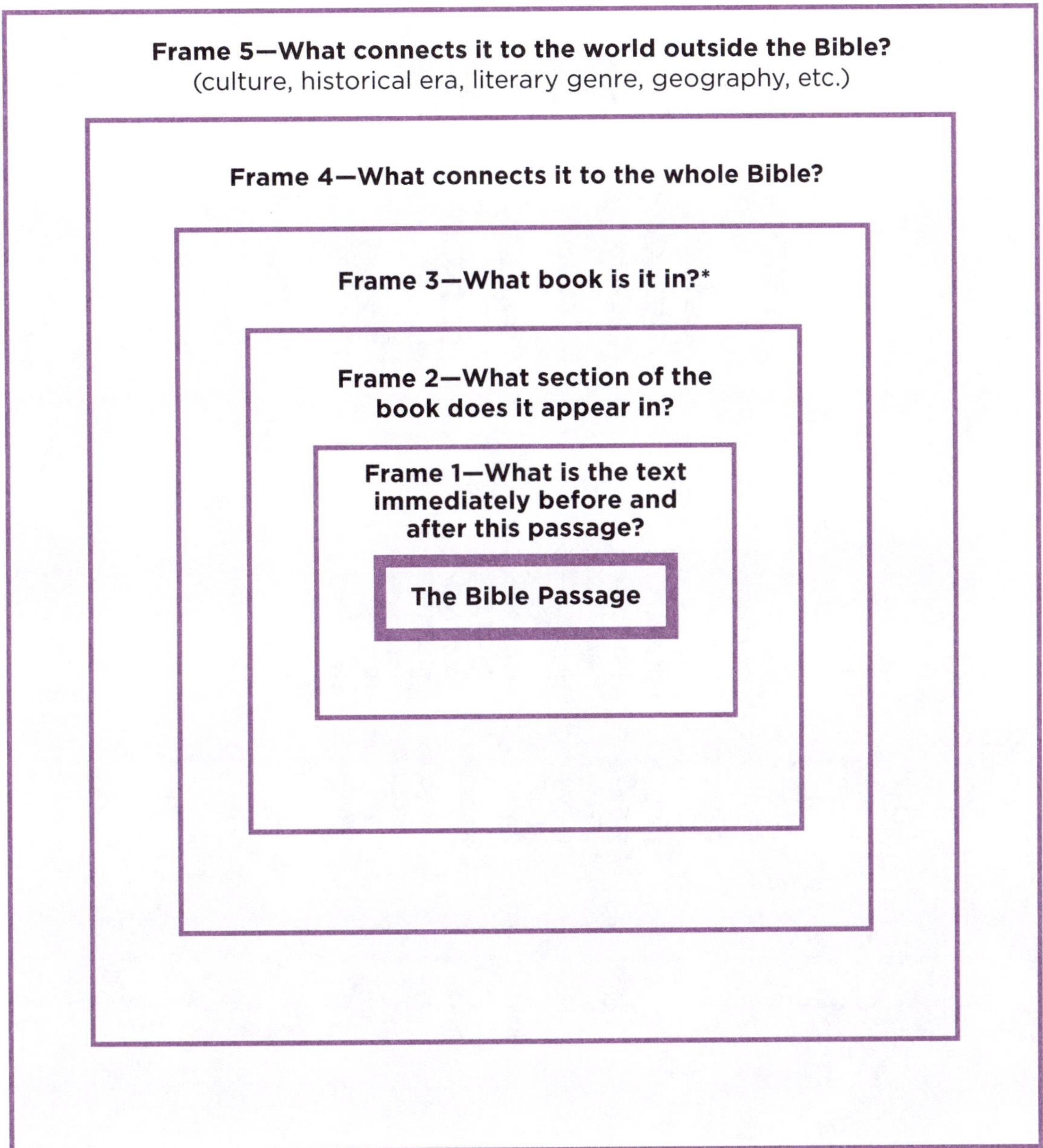

*See Appendix C

SESSION 5

CONTEXT

INDIVIDUAL PRACTICE

CONTEXT PRACTICE Day 1

Read the Scripture passage and record your CONTEXT responses to the questions that follow.

John 6:25-36

When they found him on the other side of the lake, they asked him, "Rabbi, when did you get here?"

Jesus answered, "Very truly I tell you, you are looking for me, not because you saw the signs I performed but because you ate the loaves and had your fill. Do not work for food that spoils, but for food that endures to eternal life, which the Son of Man will give you. For on him God the Father has placed his seal of approval."

Then they asked him, "What must we do to do the works God requires?"

Jesus answered, "The work of God is this: to believe in the one he has sent."

So they asked him, "What sign then will you give that we may see it and believe you? What will you do? Our ancestors ate the manna in the wilderness; as it is written: 'He gave them bread from heaven to eat.'"

Jesus said to them, "Very truly I tell you, it is not Moses who has given you the bread from heaven, but it is my Father who gives you the true bread from heaven. For the bread of God is the bread that comes down from heaven and gives life to the world."

"Sir," they said, "always give us this bread."

Then Jesus declared, "I am the bread of life. Whoever comes to me will never go hungry, and whoever believes in me will never be thirsty. But as I told you, you have seen me and still you do not believe."

What questions came up as you read this passage? Write down any questions that start with *what* or *why* here.

1.

2.

3.

4.

5.

Use the five frames to begin your search for CONTEXT for John 6:25–36. Which frame in the HOW-TO PRACTICE: CONTEXT pages 144–145 seems like it will help you answer the question you're asking?

CONTEXT FRAME I'M USING:

RESOURCE I NEED:

Explore the CONTEXT of John 6:25–36 using that frame and make notes here:

What meaning was added to John 6:25–36 from exploring its CONTEXT? How did finding CONTEXT sharpen, deepen, or change your understanding of . . .

- God?
- Yourself or humanity?
- Living a life of faith?

CONTEXT PRACTICE Day 2

Read the Scripture passage and record your CONTEXT responses to the questions that follow.

Isaiah 5:1–7

I will sing for the one I love
  a song about his vineyard:
My loved one had a vineyard
  on a fertile hillside.
He dug it up and cleared it of stones
  and planted it with the choicest vines.
He built a watchtower in it
  and cut out a winepress as well.
Then he looked for a crop of good grapes,
  but it yielded only bad fruit.

"Now you dwellers in Jerusalem and people of Judah,
  judge between me and my vineyard.
What more could have been done for my vineyard
  than I have done for it?
When I looked for good grapes,
  why did it yield only bad?
Now I will tell you
  what I am going to do to my vineyard:
I will take away its hedge,
  and it will be destroyed;
I will break down its wall,
  and it will be trampled.
I will make it a wasteland,
  neither pruned nor cultivated,
  and briers and thorns will grow there.
I will command the clouds
  not to rain on it."
The vineyard of the LORD Almighty
  is the nation of Israel,
and the people of Judah
  are the vines he delighted in.
And he looked for justice, but saw bloodshed;
  for righteousness, but heard cries of distress.

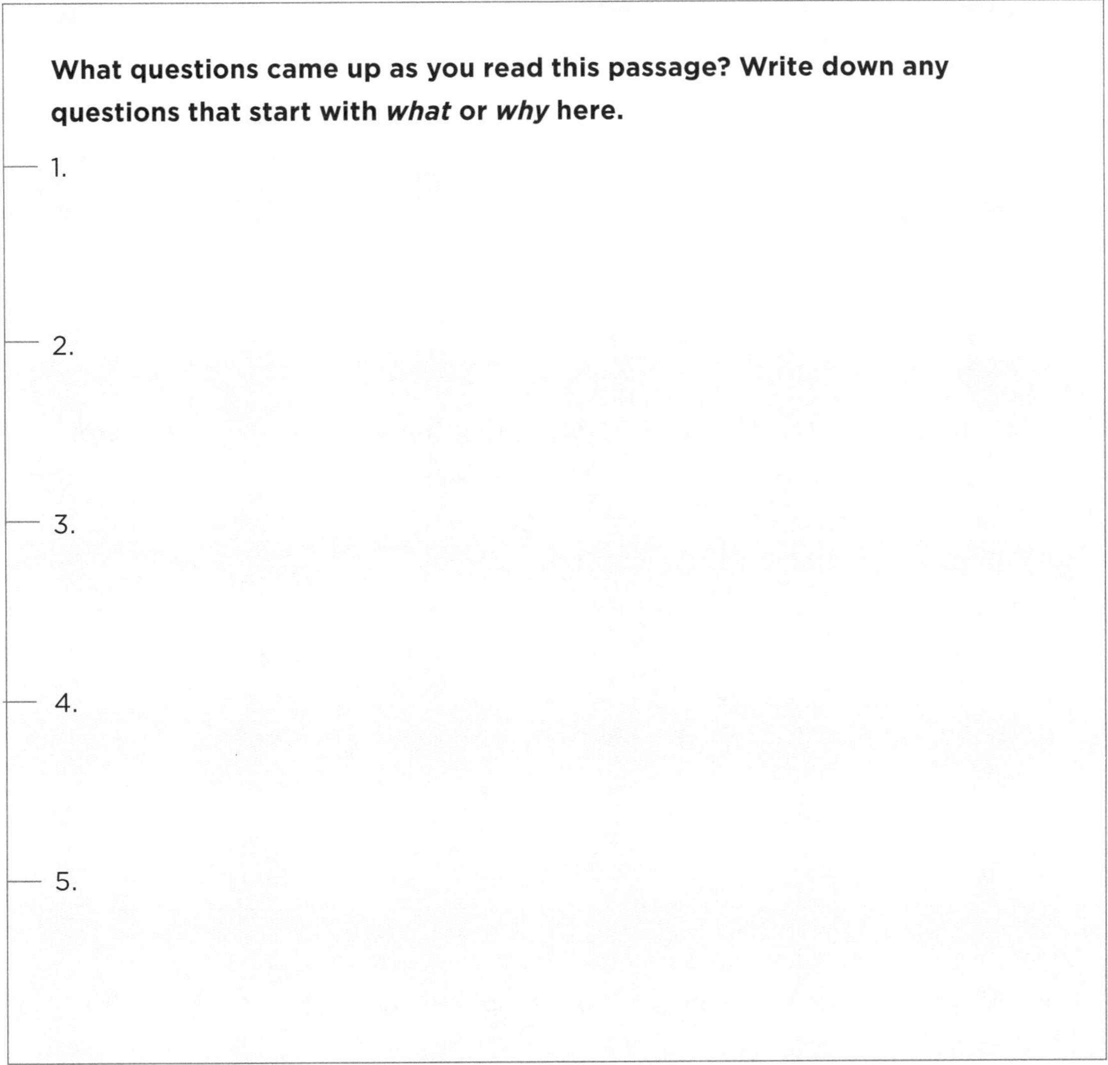

What questions came up as you read this passage? Write down any questions that start with *what* or *why* here.

1.

2.

3.

4.

5.

Use the five frames to begin your search for CONTEXT for Isaiah 5:1–7. Which frame in the HOW-TO PRACTICE: CONTEXT pages 144–145 seems like it will help you answer the question you're asking?

CONTEXT FRAME I'M USING:

RESOURCE I NEED:

Explore the CONTEXT of Isaiah 5:1–7 using that frame and make notes here:

What meaning was added to Isaiah 5:1–7 from exploring its CONTEXT? How did finding CONTEXT sharpen, deepen, or change your understanding of . . .

- God?
- Yourself or humanity?
- Living a life of faith?

CONTEXT PRACTICE Day 3

Read the Scripture passage and record your CONTEXT responses to the questions that follow.

Mark 7:24–30

Jesus left that place and went to the vicinity of Tyre. He entered a house and did not want anyone to know it; yet he could not keep his presence secret. In fact, as soon as she heard about him, a woman whose little daughter was possessed by an impure spirit came and fell at his feet. The woman was a Greek, born in Syrian Phoenicia. She begged Jesus to drive the demon out of her daughter.

"First let the children eat all they want," he told her, "for it is not right to take the children's bread and toss it to the dogs."

"Lord," she replied, "even the dogs under the table eat the children's crumbs."

Then he told her, "For such a reply, you may go; the demon has left your daughter."

She went home and found her child lying on the bed, and the demon gone.

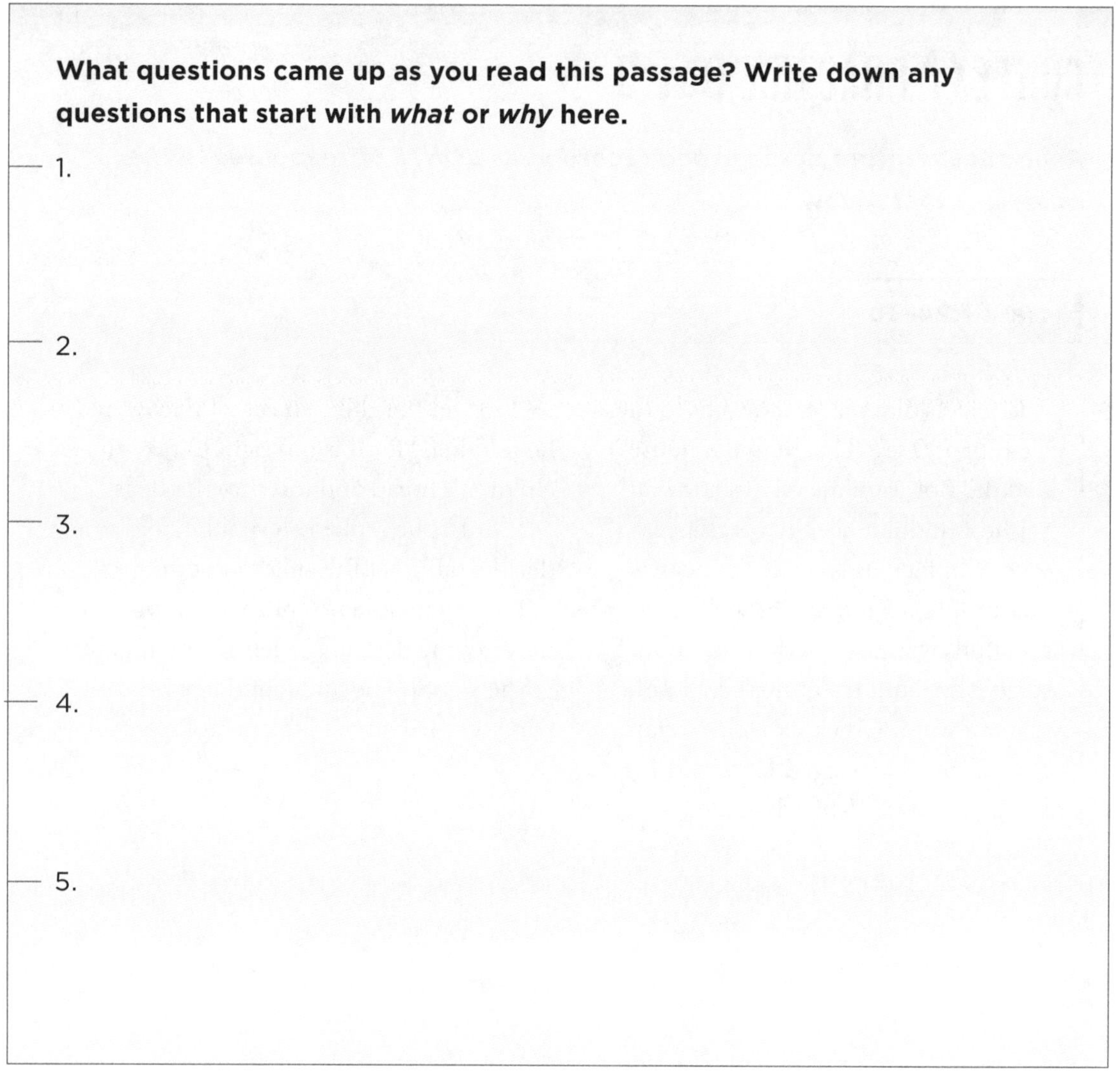

Use the five frames to begin your search for CONTEXT of Mark 7:24–30. Which frame in the HOW-TO PRACTICE: CONTEXT pages 144–145 seems like it will help you answer the question you're asking?

CONTEXT FRAME I'M USING:

RESOURCE I NEED:

Explore the CONTEXT of Mark 7:24–30 using that frame and make notes here:

What meaning was added to Mark 7:24–30 from exploring its CONTEXT? How did finding CONTEXT sharpen, deepen, or change your understanding of . . .

- God?
- Yourself or humanity?
- Living a life of faith?

Excellent work exploring the value of CONTEXT around and within every passage!

SESSION 6

ACTION

GROUP MEETING

Leader, read aloud to the group.

Welcome to *Spirit-Led Bible Study* Session 6!

This is the final week of our study, which means it's time to take all the practices you have learned and put them to work as you read the Bible week in and week out. I pray they will help you grow, but I know they won't unless you actually do them. The same is true for your entire life of faith! ACTION is the key to a faith that is strong, alive, and maturing. Simply reading your Bible is not enough; you have to follow all the way through to ACTION. So get ready to move.

ACTION is the final step in partnering with the Holy Spirit in the Word of God, as He changes you from the inside out.

"If you just use my words in Bible studies and don't work them into your life, you are like a dumb carpenter who built a house but skipped the foundation."

Luke 6:49 MSG

REVIEW SESSION 5 INDIVIDUAL PRACTICE

Leader, read these instructions aloud to the group before you begin. I recommend setting a ten-minute timer so you don't spend too much time here. You'll need most of your group time for the new practice of ACTION.

The Spirit could have led you to so many discoveries about John 6:25–36 on your Day 1 Individual Study practicing CONTEXT. Take a few minutes to share your CONTEXT findings as a group. What each person explored on their own will add to everyone's learning about this passage as a whole.

What questions came up as you read John 6:25–36? Everyone share one *what* or *why* question you had about this passage. (Remember—no question is too simple!)

Now, each person share your aha learning—one thing you discovered about the CONTEXT of this passage that added something important to the true meaning (and your understanding).

How did finding CONTEXT in John 6:25–36 sharpen, deepen, or change your understanding of . . .

- God?
- Yourself or humanity?
- Living a life of faith?

Now it's time to begin our last *Spirit-Led Bible Study* practice! You have made it to the last session.

WARM-UP

Leader, read these instructions aloud to the group before the timer begins.

Your group is going to play a game called "Shoe." I promise it won't take long and you will laugh.

HOW TO PLAY SHOE:

1. Players:
   - Designate one person the Leader. (All this person does is yell things out.)
   - Other players match up into pairs.

2. Set-up:
   - Pairs:
     - Stand facing each other about two feet apart.
     - Someone take off a shoe and put it on the floor between you.
   - Leader: Stand somewhere all pairs can hear you.

3. Gameplay:
   - Leader: Call out body parts (like "head," "knee," "eyebrow," "foot," etc.).
   - Players must touch that body part (on their own body) with both of their hands.
     - For example, if the leader calls out "elbow," players must quickly touch both elbows with both hands.
   - The leader will call out multiple body parts in a sequence, and players must keep up with the commands.
   - The leader will suddenly yell "Shoe!" (instead of a body part).
   - All players must immediately try to grab the shoe between them.

4. Winning:
   - The player in each pair who grabs the shoe first is the winner of that round.

- All winners find a new partner and play the next round.
- Continue playing as many rounds as it takes to get one winner.
- If you grab the shoe in the final matchup, then congrats—you won Shoe!
- (Now, everyone put their shoes back on.)

After the game, discuss how the three parts of the game are similar to three necessities in living a life of faith. To be involved in both, you must:

- Decide to engage
- LISTEN to the words being spoken
- Actually DO what is said

Everyone share: Which of these three things do you find hardest to do in your faith right now?

WORD OF ENCOURAGEMENT FROM ALLI

Leader, read this aloud or select a volunteer to read to the group.

I've never been into fads (though I will admit that I wore some really tacky Jams shorts in the eighties). I am drawn to what my football-loving husband would call a "blocking and tackling" mindset. I like to get the basics right and set foundations in place. I don't play football, but I guess blocking and tackling are basic necessities of being a good football team. Can't win without them! However, they're not sexy, and it's easy to favor flashier aspects of the game. That's all true in a life of faith as well. There are plenty of spiritual fads, new and exciting preachers, and the latest book about how to find peace. But you will never meet someone with strong, lasting faith in Christ who has not learned to do three things: connect personally with Jesus, deeply engage the Bible, and take real ACTIONS to follow the Word in everyday life. You just can't get around these foundations if you want a lasting faith. The last one—ACTION—is how faith becomes real. It's how you own what's in the pages of the Bible for yourself. If you never move, you might believe correct things, but your faith won't last.

You are called to a life of vibrant, even risky, ACTION to follow Jesus. In the parable of the wise and foolish builders in Luke 6 and Matthew 7, Jesus essentially says the same thing: If you want a faith and a life that stands, you have to actually do what the Word says! The rock-solid parts of my own faith are the ones set in place when I have done what the Word says. So, get ready. Let's do this.

NOW IT'S TIME TO TURN ON THE SESSION 6 VIDEO.

WATCH SESSION 6 VIDEO

Leader, stream the video or play the DVD.

ACTION PRACTICE NOTES

Capture anything you want to remember about this practice as you watch the video. These notes will help you when you ACT as a group and on your own.

ACTION + Accountability

"So let's *do* it—full of belief, confident that we're presentable inside and out. Let's keep a firm grip on the promises that keep us going. He always keeps his word. Let's see how inventive we can be in encouraging love and helping out, not avoiding worshiping together as some do but spurring each other on, especially as we see the big Day approaching." —Hebrews 10:22–25 MSG

Choose an Accountability Partner and Talk About:

- What exactly do you need to be held accountable to do?
- How often will the other person check in? (daily, weekly, etc.)
- What is your preferred check-in format? (texts, calls, in-person, app)
- What happens if you miss goals? (gentle reminders, pep talks, do it together, etc.)

Ask:

- What is God's job, role, or responsibility?
- What is my job, role, or responsibility?

Act:

- What action will you take?
- Make a plan of action.
- Set goals for action.

Leader, invite the Holy Spirit into your group practice, and the prompts aloud to your group.

COME TO JESUS

Write one honest thing to Him, as if you are speaking to Him directly.

Confess one thing that is in the way of your coming to Him or in the way as you come to Him.

Tell Him you are here and open.

HEAR HIS WORD

Leader, read the passage aloud to the group.

1 Peter 2:11–17

Dear friends, I urge you, as foreigners and exiles, to abstain from sinful desires, which wage war against your soul. Live such good lives among the pagans that, though they accuse you of doing wrong, they may see your good deeds and glorify God on the day he visits us.

Submit yourselves for the Lord's sake to every human authority: whether to the emperor, as the supreme authority, or to governors, who are sent by him to punish those who do wrong and to commend those who do right. For it is God's will that by doing good you should silence the ignorant talk of foolish people. Live as free people, but do not use your freedom as a cover-up for evil; live as God's slaves. Show proper respect to everyone, love the family of believers, fear God, honor the emperor.

Circle the parts of this passage that indicate *God's* job/role/ACTION/ responsibility.

Underline the parts of this passage that indicate *your* job/role/ACTION/ responsibility.

PUT IT INTO PRACTICE

What part of the Word is the Spirit highlighting to you today?

What ACTION could you take that would send God the message that you heard this word?

TIME'S UP!

Return now to the video for a short wrap-up of this practice from Alli.

GROUP DISCUSSION

Leader, read each prompt to the group for deeper discussion. Do not be concerned if you don't make it through every question. Trust the Spirit to lead your discussion as your group needs, so that you can connect and grow.

1. Briefly share if/how your experience of the Holy Spirit has changed your personal Bible study over the past five weeks.
2. Do you see yourself as a person of ACTION? Has that been true in response to the things you read in the Bible? Share an example.
3. Discuss how obedience and ACTION are the same, and share any differences that you might see.
4. Alli taught that coming to Jesus in honesty, humility, and confession is the first step in the practice of ACTION. In what ways does a simple conversation with Jesus through the Holy Spirit affect your response to Scripture?
5. What would change in your Bible study if you believe that God meant for you to ACT in some way?
6. What do you notice in your spirit as you consider God's desire for ACTION in your life? (Do you feel a stirring challenge? Excitement? Pressure? Overwhelm?)
7. In our group practice, how did ACTION sharpen, deepen, or change your understanding of...
    - God?
    - Yourself or humanity?
    - Living a life of faith?

PREP FOR INDIVIDUAL STUDY

Leader, read this to the group.

This week you will read and respond to a few passages of Scripture on your own while practicing ACTION. On the following pages, you will find a reference chart for how to practice ACTION well. I encourage you to dive into this practice with your whole heart and ask the Holy Spirit to shape you, stretch you, and grow you as you do. My greatest prayer for you is that you will find each of these practices useful in your Bible study from here on—and that ACTION will become the natural outflow of all your Bible engagement and your response to the Holy Spirit!

CLOSING PRAYER

Leader, read this prayer over your group before dismissing.

Lord, move me to a deeper life of faith. I repent of all the times I have read my Bible and done nothing in my real life with its words. I want to be someone who follows You daily. Help me stand firm in the face of resistance and mature my faith in You at any cost. In Jesus' name,

Amen

HOW-TO PRACTICE: ACTION

COME TO JESUS

- Say one honest thing to Him, as if you are speaking to Him directly.
- Confess anything that is in the way of your coming to Him or in the way as you come to Him.
- Tell Him you are here and open.

HEAR HIS WORD

- Put this passage into your own words.
- What part of this passage indicates **God's job**/role/action/responsibility?
- What part of this passage indicates **your job**/role/action/responsibility?

PUT IT INTO PRACTICE

- What part of the Word is the Spirit highlighting to you today?

- **What ACTION could you take that would send God the message that you heard this word?**

- What "experiment" might help you move/act, even if you are not sure?

- What resistance might you expect to face?

SESSION 6

ACTION

INDIVIDUAL PRACTICE

We've finally reached our final time of personal practice. This week, as you practice ACTION on your own, consider the other practices you have learned over the past six weeks as well. I challenge you to sit with the Holy Spirit and seek His guidance for where, how, and in what specific ways you can let Him lead your Bible study through these practices as you go from this experience.

It has been more than a joy to walk you through these practices and share what has shaped and stretched and grown my own faith over the years. The Bible is alive. It is waiting for our engagement, and it will never return void. Trust the Spirit who inspired every word on the pages of Scripture, and He will always lead you deeper, closer, wiser, and more sure of just how great the love of our Father is!

ACTION PRACTICE Day 1

COME TO JESUS

Say one honest thing to Him, as if you are speaking to Him directly.

Confess anything that is in the way of your coming to Him or in the way as you come to Him.

Tell Him you are here and open.

HEAR HIS WORD

Romans 12:9–21

Love must be sincere. Hate what is evil; cling to what is good. Be devoted to one another in love. Honor one another above yourselves. Never be lacking in zeal, but keep your spiritual fervor, serving the Lord. Be joyful in hope, patient in affliction, faithful in prayer. Share with the Lord's people who are in need. Practice hospitality.

Bless those who persecute you; bless and do not curse. Rejoice with those who rejoice; mourn with those who mourn. Live in harmony with one another. Do not be proud, but be willing to associate with people of low position. Do not be conceited.

Do not repay anyone evil for evil. Be careful to do what is right in the eyes of everyone. If it is possible, as far as it depends on you, live at peace with everyone. Do not take revenge, my dear friends, but leave room for God's wrath, for it is written: "It is mine to avenge; I will repay," says the Lord. On the contrary:

"If your enemy is hungry, feed him;
if he is thirsty, give him something to drink.
In doing this, you will heap burning coals on his head."

Do not be overcome by evil, but overcome evil with good.

Put this passage into your own words.

What part of this passage indicates **God's job**/role/ACTION/responsibility?

What part of this passage indicates **your job**/role/ACTION/responsibility?

PUT IT INTO PRACTICE

What part of the Word is the Spirit highlighting to you today?

What ACTION could you take that would send God the message that you heard this word?

What "experiment" might help you move, even if you are not sure?

What resistance might you expect to face?

How did putting Romans 12:9–21 into ACTION sharpen, deepen, or change your understanding of . . .

- God?
- Yourself or humanity?
- Living a life of faith?

ACTION PRACTICE Day 2

COME TO JESUS

Say one honest thing to Him, as if you are speaking to Him directly.

Confess anything that is in the way of your coming to Him or in the way as you come to Him.

Tell Him you are here and open.

HEAR HIS WORD

Proverbs 3:1–10

My son, do not forget my teaching,
  but keep my commands in your heart,
for they will prolong your life many years
  and bring you peace and prosperity.
Let love and faithfulness never leave you;
  bind them around your neck,
  write them on the tablet of your heart.
Then you will win favor and a good name
  in the sight of God and man.

> Trust in the Lord with all your heart
> and lean not on your own understanding;
> in all your ways submit to him,
> and he will make your paths straight.
> Do not be wise in your own eyes;
> fear the Lord and shun evil.
> This will bring health to your body
> and nourishment to your bones.
> Honor the Lord with your wealth,
> with the firstfruits of all your crops;
> then your barns will be filled to overflowing,
> and your vats will brim over with new wine.

Put this passage into your own words.

What part of this passage indicates **God's job**/role/ACTION/responsibility?

What part of this passage indicates **your job**/role/ACTION/responsibility?

What part of the Word is the Spirit highlighting to you today?

PUT IT INTO PRACTICE

What ACTION could you take that would send God the message that you heard this word?

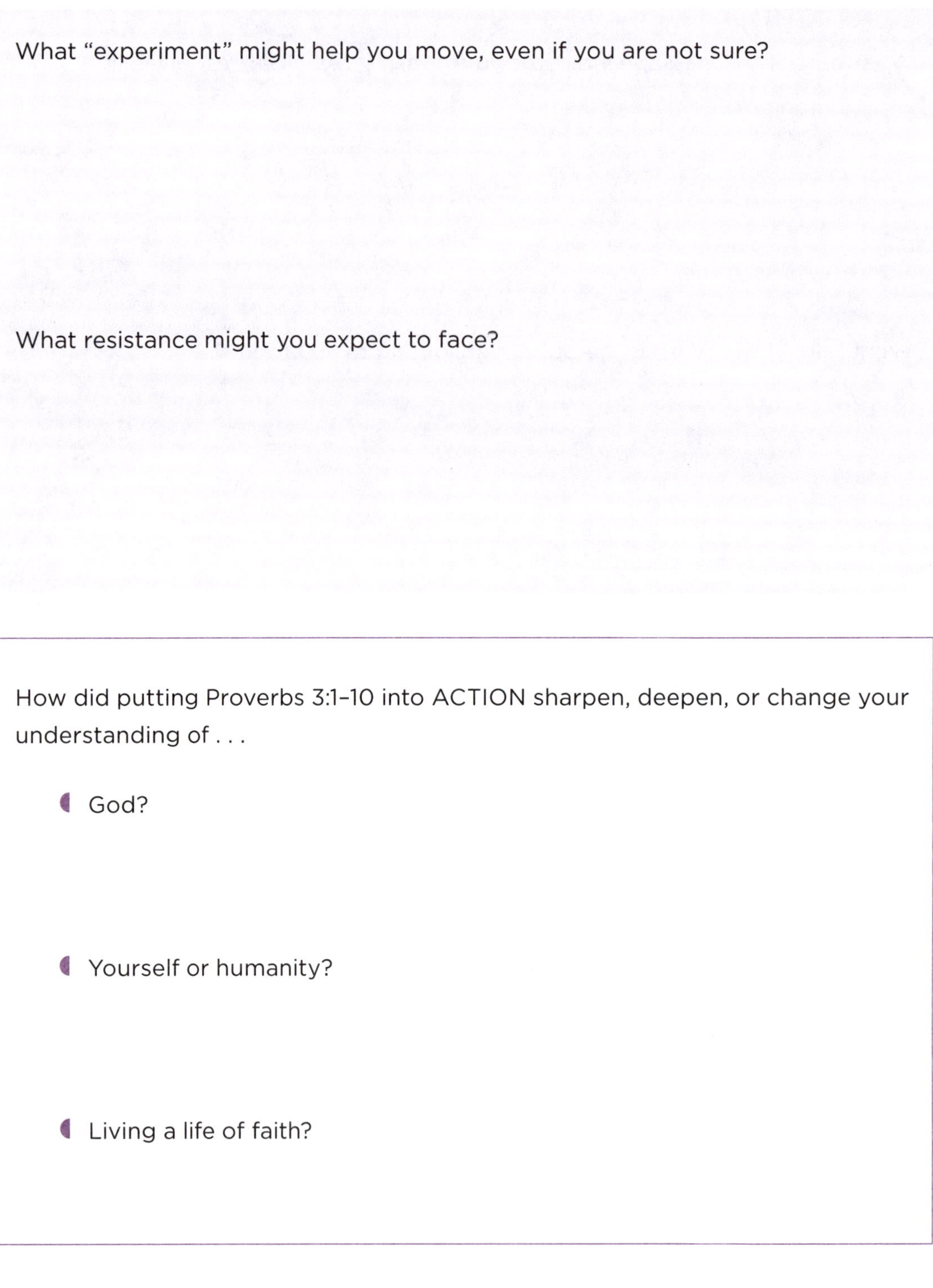

What "experiment" might help you move, even if you are not sure?

What resistance might you expect to face?

How did putting Proverbs 3:1–10 into ACTION sharpen, deepen, or change your understanding of . . .

- God?
- Yourself or humanity?
- Living a life of faith?

ACTION PRACTICE Day 3

COME TO JESUS

Say one honest thing to Him, as if you are speaking to Him directly.

Confess anything that is in the way of your coming to Him or in the way as you come to Him.

Tell Him you are here and open.

HEAR HIS WORD

Matthew 5:11–16

"Blessed are you when people insult you, persecute you and falsely say all kinds of evil against you because of me. Rejoice and be glad, because great is your reward in heaven, for in the same way they persecuted the prophets who were before you.

"You are the salt of the earth. But if the salt loses its saltiness, how can it be made salty again? It is no longer good for anything, except to be thrown out and trampled underfoot.

"You are the light of the world. A town built on a hill cannot be hidden. Neither do people light a lamp and put it under a bowl. Instead they put it on its stand, and it gives light to everyone in the house. In the same way, let your light shine before others, that they may see your good deeds and glorify your Father in heaven."

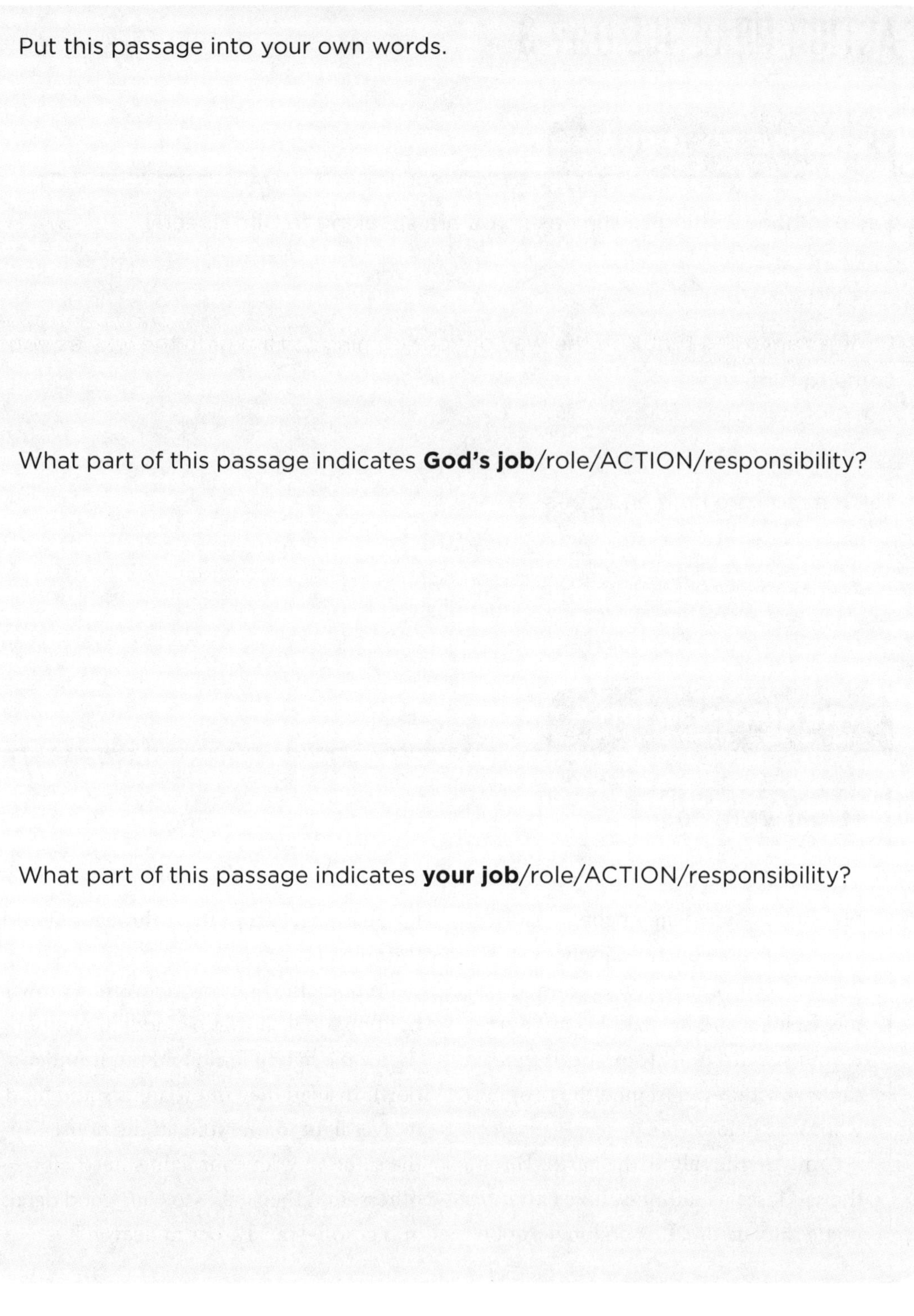

Put this passage into your own words.

What part of this passage indicates **God's job**/role/ACTION/responsibility?

What part of this passage indicates **your job**/role/ACTION/responsibility?

PUT IT INTO PRACTICE

What part of the Word is the Spirit highlighting to you today?

What ACTION could you take that would send God the message that you heard this word?

What "experiment" might help you move, even if you are not sure?

What resistance might you expect to face?

How did putting Matthew 5:11–16 into ACTION sharpen, deepen, or change your understanding of . . .

- God?

- Yourself or humanity?

- Living a life of faith?

Well Done! My prayer and hope is that you feel equipped to move from the pages of Scripture into ACTION!

MY FINAL ENCOURAGEMENT

Schedule one last group gathering to celebrate this time you've spent seeking and growing together! (Bonus points if you review your Individual Practice from Session 6!)

My hope and final blessing for you is rooted in Psalm 119:105:

May the Word of God always be the lamp for your feet and the light on your path.

I hope *Spirit-Led Bible Study* will continue to bring your Bible to life and that the Spirit will continue to lead you inside and outside the pages of God's Word.

In Christ, Alli

ABOUT THE AUTHOR

Alli Patterson is a teacher, author, wife and mom of four out of Cincinnati, Ohio. She currently serves as a Teaching Pastor at Crossroads Church on the national teaching team. Alli is the leader of Woman Camp and founder of the Ignite Conference out of her passion for equipping women in the Kingdom of God.

As a lifetime learner and lover of scripture with a seminary degree from Dallas Theological Seminary, Alli loves to create ways for others to know and love Jesus through his Word. She has created a fresh approach to Bible study in the release of 'Spirit-Led Bible Study,' coming February 2026. She has written two books, How to Stay Standing and Blueprint for Belonging - both providing practical help translating Biblical principles into real life. Alli speaks at events and conferences and enjoys podcasting. She is a runner and die hard Buckeye football fan who loves Mexican food almost as much as her bratty calico cat.

Website - https://www.allipatterson.com/
Instagram/Facebook - @theallipatterson

APPENDIX A

Jonah's Travels

APPENDIX B Common Biblical Verbs to Use in Prayer

VERBS	EXAMPLES
A - ASK, ANOINT, ABIDE	"Ask and it will be given" (Matt. 7:7); "Anoint him" (1 Sam. 16:12); "Abide in Me" (John 15:4 NKJV).
B - BELIEVE, BAPTIZE, BLESS	"Believe in the Lord" (Acts 16:31); "Baptizing them . . ." (Matt. 28:19); "Bless those who curse you" (Luke 6:28).
C - CREATE, CONFESS, COME	"God created the heavens" (Gen. 1:1), "Confess your sins" (James 5:16), "Come to me" (Matt. 11:28).
D - DELIVER, DO, DWELL	"Deliver us from evil" (Matt. 6:13 NASB); "Do not fear" (Isa. 41:10); "Dwell in the house of the Lord" (Ps. 23:6).
E - EAT, ENTER, ENCOURAGE	"Eat from it" (Gen. 3:5); "Enter his gates" (Ps. 100:4); "Encourage one another" (1 Thess. 5:11).
F - FORGIVE, FOLLOW, FEAR	"Forgive them" (Luke 23:34); "Follow me" (Matt. 4:19); "Fear God" (Eccl. 12:13).
G - GIVE, GO, GLORIFY	"Give thanks" (1 Thess. 5:18); "Go into all the world" (Mark 16:15); "Glorify your Father" (Matt. 5:16).
H - HEAR, HELP, HUMBLE	"Hear, O Israel" (Deut. 6:4); "The Sovereign Lord helps me" (Isa. 50:7); "Humble yourselves" (James 4:10).
I - INHERIT, INTERCEDE, INCREASE	"Inherit the kingdom" (Matt. 25:34 NKJV); "Christ . . . intercedes for us" (Rom. 8:34 NASB); "Increase our faith" (Luke 17:5).
J - JUDGE, JUSTIFY, JOIN	"Judge not" (Matt. 7:1 NKJV); "Justified by faith" (Rom. 5:1 NKJV); "Joined to the Lord" (1 Cor. 6:17 NKJV).

K - KEEP, KNEEL, KNOW "Keep My commandments" (John 14:15 NKJV); "Kneel before the LORD" (Ps. 95:6); "Know that I am God" (Ps. 46:10).

L - LOVE, LISTEN, LEARN "Love your neighbor" (Matt. 22:39); "Listen to Him!" (Matt. 17:5 NASB); "Learn from me" (Matt. 11:29).

M - MEDITATE, MAKE, MINISTER "Meditate on it" (Josh. 1:8); "Make disciples" (Matt. 28:19); "Minister . . . to the saints" (Heb. 6:10 NKJV).

N - NAME, NURTURE, NEGLECT (NOT) "Name Him Jesus" (Matt. 1:21 NASB); "Nurture and admonition" (Eph. 6:4 KJV); "Let us not neglect" (Heb. 10:25 NLT).

O - OBEY, OFFER, OVERCOME "Obey the LORD your God" (Deut. 28:1); "Offer your bodies" (Rom. 12:1); "Overcome evil with good" (Rom. 12:21).

P - PRAY, PREACH, PRAISE "Pray without ceasing" (1 Thess. 5:17 NKJV); "Preach the word" (2 Tim. 4:2); "Praise the LORD" (Ps. 150:1).

Q - QUENCH, QUESTION, QUIET (BE) "Do not quench the Spirit" (1 Thess. 5:19); "Why do you question this in your hearts?" (Mark 2:8 NLT); "Quiet!" (Mark 4:39).

R - REPENT, REJOICE, RUN "Repent, for the kingdom . . ." (Matt. 3:2); "Rejoice in the Lord" (Phil. 4:4); "Run with perseverance" (Heb. 12:1).

S - SEEK, SERVE, SPEAK "Seek first his kingdom" (Matt. 6:33); "Serv[e] the Lord" (Rom. 12:11); "Speak . . . the truth" (Eph. 4:15).

T - TRUST, TEACH, TAKE "Trust in the LORD" (Prov. 3:5); "Teach . . . them to obey" (Matt. 28:20); "Take up your cross" (Luke 9:23 NLT).

U - UNDERSTAND, USE, UNITE	"Understand what the will of the Lord is" (Eph. 5:17 NKJV); "Use [your] gift[s]" (1 Peter 4:10); "United in mind" (1 Cor. 1:10).
V - VISIT, VINDICATE, VALUE	"Visit orphans and widows" (James 1:27 NKJV); "The LORD will vindicate me" (Ps. 138:8); "You are more valuable" (Matt. 10:31 NLT).
W - WORSHIP, WAIT, WALK	"Worship the Lord" (Matt. 4:10); "Wait on the LORD" (Isa. 40:31 NKJV); "Walk in the Spirit" (Gal. 5:16 NKJV).
X - EXALT, EXAMINE, EXECUTE	"Exalt the LORD" (Ps. 99:5); "Examine yourselves" (2 Cor. 13:5); "Execute true justice" (Zech. 7:9 NKJV).
Y - YIELD, YOKE, YEARN	"Yield yourselves to God" (Rom. 6:13 AMPC); "Take my yoke upon you" (Matt. 11:29); "My soul yearns for you" (Isa. 26:9).
Z - ZEAL (BE ZEALOUS), ZAP	"Be zealous" (Rev. 3:19 NKJV); "He will strike [symbolic for judgment] the earth" (Isa. 11:4).

APPENDIX C Harmony of the Gospels

DATE	EVENT	LOCATION	MATTHEW	MARK	LUKE	JOHN
INTRODUCTIONS TO JESUS CHRIST						
	(1) Luke's introduction				1:1–4	
	(2) Preincarnate Christ					1:1–18
	(3) Genealogy of Jesus Christ		1:1–17		3:23b–38	
BIRTH, INFANCY, AND ADOLESCENCE OF JESUS AND JOHN THE BAPTIST						
7 **BC**	(1) Announcement of birth of John	Jerusalem (temple)			1:5–25	
7 or 6 **BC**	(2) Announcement of birth of Jesus to the virgin Mary	Nazareth			1:26–38	
ca. 5 **BC**	(3) Song of Elizabeth to Mary	Hill country of Judea			1:39–45	
	(4) Mary's song of praise				1:46–56	
5 **BC**	(5) Birth, infancy, and purpose for future of John the Baptist	Judea			1:57–80	
	(6) Announcement of Jesus' birth to Joseph	Nazareth	1:18–25a			
5–4 **BC**	(7) Birth of Jesus Christ	Bethlehem	1:25b		2:1–7	
	(8) Proclamation by the angels	Near Bethlehem			2:8–14	
	(9) The visit of homage by shepherds	Bethlehem			2:15–20	
	(10) Jesus' circumcision	Bethlehem			2:21	
4 **BC**	(11) First temple visit with acknowledgments by Simeon and Anna	Jerusalem			2:22–38	
	(12) Visit of the Magi	Jerusalem & Bethlehem	2:1–12			
	(13) Flight into Egypt and massacre of innocents	Bethlehem, Jerusalem & Egypt	2:13–18			
	(14) From Egypt to Nazareth with Jesus		2:19–23		2:39	
Afterward **AD** 7–8	(15) Childhood of Jesus	Nazareth			2:40	
	(16) Jesus, 12 years old, visits the temple	Jerusalem			2:41–50	
Afterward	(17) 18-year account of Jesus' adolescence and adulthood	Nazareth			2:51–52	
TRUTHS ABOUT JOHN THE BAPTIST						
ca. **AD** 25–27	(1) John's ministry begins	Judean Wilderness	3:1	1:1–4	3:1–2	1:19–28
	(2) Man and message		3:2–12	1:2–8	3:3–14	1:20–23
	(3) His picture of Jesus		3:11–12	1:7–8	3:15–18	1:24–27
	(4) His courage		14:4–12		3:19–20	
BEGINNING OF JESUS' MINISTRY						
ca. **AD** 27	(1) Jesus baptized	Jordan River	3:13–17	1:9–11	3:21–23a	1:29–34
	(2) Jesus tempted	Wilderness	4:1–11	1:12–13	4:1–13	
	(3) Calls first disciples	Beyond Jordan				1:35–51
	(4) The first miracle	Cana in Galilee				2:1–11

DATE	EVENT	LOCATION	MATTHEW	MARK	LUKE	JOHN
BEGINNING OF JESUS' MINISTRY (CONT.)						
AD 27	(5) First stay in Capernaum	(Capernaum is "his" city)				2:12
	(6) First cleansing of the temple	Jerusalem				2:13–22
	(7) Received at Jerusalem	Jerusalem				2:23–25
	(8) Teaches Nicodemus about second birth	Jerusalem				3:1–21
	(9) Co-ministry with John	Judea				3:22–36
	(10) Leaves for Galilee	Judea	4:12	1:14	4:14	4:1–4
	(11) Samaritan woman at Jacob's Well	Samaria (town of Sychar)				4:5–42
	(12) Returns to Galilee			1:15	4:15	4:43–45
THE GALILEAN MINISTRY OF JESUS						
AD 27–29						
AD 27	(1) Healing of the royal official's son	Cana				4:46–54
	(2) Rejected at Nazareth	Nazareth			4:16–30	
	(3) Moved to Capernaum	Capernaum	4:13–17			
	(4) Four become fishers of people	Sea of Galilee	4:18–22	1:16–20	5:1–11	
	(5) Impure spirit driven out on the Sabbath day	Capernaum		1:21–28	4:31–37	
	(6) Peter's mother-in-law cured, plus others	Capernaum	8:14–17	1:29–34	4:38–41	
ca. AD 27	(7) First preaching tour of Galilee	Galilee	4:23–25	1:35–39	4:42–44	
	(8) Leper healed and response recorded	Galilee	8:1–4	1:40–45	5:12–16	
	(9) Paralyzed man healed	Capernaum	9:1–8	2:1–12	5:17–26	
	(10) Matthew's call and reception held	Capernaum	9:9–13	2:13–17	5:27–32	
	(11) Disciples defended via a parable	Capernaum	9:14–17	2:18–22	5:33–39	
AD 28	(12) Goes to Jerusalem for second passover; heals lame man	Jerusalem				5:1–47
	(13) Plucked grain precipitates Sabbath controversy	En route to Galilee	12:1–8	2:23–28	6:1–5	
	(14) Shriveled hand healed causes another Sabbath controversy	Galilee	12:9–14	3:1–6	6:6–11	
	(15) Multitudes healed	Sea of Galilee	12:15–21	3:7–12	6:17–19	
	(16) Twelve apostles selected after a night of prayer	Near Capernaum		3:13–19	6:12–16	
	(17) Sermon on the Mount	Near Capernaum	5:1—7:29		6:20–49	
	(18) Centurion's servant healed	Capernaum	8:5–13		7:1–10	
	(19) Raises widow's son from the dead	Nain			7:11–17	
	(20) Jesus allays John the Baptist's doubts	Galilee	11:2–19		7:18–35	

DATE	EVENT	LOCATION	MATTHEW	MARK	LUKE	JOHN
THE GALILEAN MINISTRY OF JESUS (CONT.)						
AD 28	(21) Woes upon the privileged		11:20–30			
	(22) A sinful woman anoints Jesus	Simon the Pharisee's house, Capernaum			7:36–50	
	(23) Another tour of Galilee	Galilee			8:1–3	
	(24) Jesus accused of blasphemy	Capernaum	12:22–37	3:20–30	11:14–23	
	(25) Jesus' answer to a demand for a sign	Capernaum	12:38–45		11:24–26, 29–36	
	(26) Mother, brothers seek audience	Capernaum	12:46–50	3:31–35	8:19–21	
	(27) Famous parables of sower, seed, weeds, lamp, mustard seed, yeast, treasure, pearl, net, told	By Sea of Galilee	13:1–52	4:1–34	8:4–18	
	(28) Sea made serene	Sea of Galilee	8:23–27	4:35–41	8:22–25	
	(29) Gadarene (Gerasene) demon-possessed men healed	Eastern shore of Galilee	8:28–34	5:1–20	8:26–39	
	(30) Jairus's daughter raised and woman with hemorrhage healed		9:18–26	5:21–43	8:40–56	
	(31) Two blind men's sight restored		9:27–31			
	(32) Mute demon-possessed man healed		9:32–34			
	(33) Nazareth's second rejection of Christ	Nazareth	13:53–58	6:1–6		
	(34) Twelve sent out		9:35—11:1	6:7–13	9:1–6	
	(35) Fearful Herod beheads John the Baptist	Galilee	14:1–12	6:14–29	9:7–9	
Spring **AD** 29	(36) Return of 12, Jesus withdraws, 5,000 fed	Near Bethsaida	14:13–21	6:30–44	9:10–17	6:1–15
	(37) Walks on the water	Sea of Galilee	14:22–33	6:45–52		6:16–21
	(38) Sick people healed in Gennesaret	Gennesaret	14:34–36	6:53–56		
	(39) Peak of popularity passes in Galilee	Capernaum				6:22—7:1
AD 29	(40) Traditions attacked		15:1–20	7:1–23		
	(41) Aborted retirement in Tyre: Syrophoenician's daughter healed	Tyre	15:21–28	7:24–30		
	(42) Afflicted healed	Decapolis	15:29–31	7:31–37		
	(43) 4,000 fed	Decapolis	15:32–39	8:1–9		
	(44) Pharisees increase attack	Magadan	16:1–4	8:10–13		
	(45) Disciples' carelessness condemned; blind man healed		16:5–12	8:14–26		
	(46) Peter confesses Jesus is the Christ	Near Caesarea Philippi	16:13–20	8:27–30	9:18–21	
	(47) Jesus foretells his death	Caesarea Philippi	16:21–26	8:31–38	9:22–25	

DATE	EVENT	LOCATION	MATTHEW	MARK	LUKE	JOHN
THE GALILEAN MINISTRY OF JESUS (CONT.)						
AD 29	(48) Kingdom promised		16:27–28	9:1	9:26–27	
	(49) The transfiguration	Mountain unnamed	17:1–13	9:2–13	9:28–36	
	(50) Demon-possessed boy healed	Mount of Transfiguration	17:14–21	9:14–29	9:37–42	
	(51) Again tells of death, resurrection	Galilee	17:22–23	9:30–32	9:43–45	
	(52) Taxes paid	Capernaum	17:24–27			
	(53) Disciples contend about greatness; Jesus defines it; also patience, loyalty, forgiveness	Capernaum	18:1–35	9:33–50	9:46–50	
	(54) Jesus rejects his brothers' advice	Galilee				7:2–9
Fall **AD** 29	(55) Galilee departure and Samaritan rejection		19:1–2		9:51–56	7:10
	(56) Cost of discipleship		8:18–22		9:57–62	
LAST JUDEAN AND PEREAN MINISTRY OF JESUS						
AD 29–30						
Fall **AD** 29	(1) Festival of Tabernacles	Jerusalem				7:2,11–52
	(2) Forgiveness of woman caught in the act of adultery	Jerusalem				[7:53—8:11]
AD 29	(3) Christ—the light of the world	Jerusalem				8:12
	(4) Pharisees dispute the prophet's words and thus try to destroy him	Jerusalem—temple				8:13–59
	(5) Man born blind healed; following consequences	Jerusalem				9:1–41
	(6) Parable of the Good Shepherd	Jerusalem				10:1–21
	(7) The service of the 72	Probably Judea			10:1–24	
	(8) Expert in the law hears the story of the Good Samaritan	Judea (?)			10:25–37	
	(9) The hospitality of Martha and Mary	Bethany			10:38–42	
	(10) Another lesson on prayer	Judea (?)			11:1–13	
	(11) Accused of connection with Beelzebul				11:14–36	
	(12) Judgment against pharisees and experts in the law				11:37–54	
	(13) Jesus deals with hypocrisy, greed, worry, and watchfulness				12:1–59	
	(14) Repent or perish				13:1–5	
	(15) Barren fig tree				13:6–9	
	(16) Crippled woman healed on Sabbath				13:10–17	
	(17) Parables of mustard seed and yeast	Probably Perea			13:18–21	

DATE	EVENT	LOCATION	MATTHEW	MARK	LUKE	JOHN
LAST JUDEAN AND PEREAN MINISTRY OF JESUS (CONT.)						
Winter **AD** 29	(18) Festival of Dedication	Jerusalem				10:22–39
	(19) Withdrawal beyond Jordan					10:40–42
	(20) Jesus teaches, with special words about Herod	Perea			13:22–35	
	(21) Meal with a Pharisee ruler; heals man with abnormal swelling; parables of ox, best places at the table, and great banquet				14:1–24	
	(22) Demands of discipleship	Perea			14:25–35	
	(23) Parables of lost sheep, coin, son				15:1–32	
	(24) Parables of shrewd manager, rich man and Lazarus				16:1–31	
	(25) Lessons on forgiveness, duty, influence, faith				17:1–10	
	(26) Resurrection of Lazarus	Perea to Bethany				11:1–44
	(27) Reaction to resurrection of Lazarus: withdrawal of Jesus					11:45–54
AD 30	(28) Begins last journey to Jerusalem via Samaria & Galilee	Samaria, Galilee			17:11	
	(29) Heals ten lepers				17:12–19	
	(30) Lessons on the coming kingdom				17:20–37	
	(31) Parables: persistent widow, Pharisee and tax collector				18:1–14	
	(32) Teaching on divorce		19:3–12	10:1–12		
	(33) Jesus blesses children; objections	Perea	19:13–15	10:13–16	18:15–17	
	(34) Rich ruler	Perea	19:16–30	10:17–31	18:18–30	
	(35) Parable of the workers		20:1–16			
	(36) Foretells death and resurrection	Near Jerusalem	20:17–19	10:32–34	18:31–34	
	(37) Ambition of James and John		20:20–28	10:35–45		
	(38) Blind Bartimaeus and his companion healed	Jericho	20:29–34	10:46–52	18:35–43	
	(39) Interview with Zacchaeus	Jericho			19:1–10	
	(40) Parable of the minas	Jericho			19:11–27	
	(41) Returns to home of Mary and Martha	Bethany				11:55—12:1
	(42) Plot to kill Lazarus	Bethany				12:9–11
JESUS' FINAL WEEK AROUND AND IN JERUSALEM						
Spring **AD** 30						
Sunday	(1) Triumphal Entry	Bethany, Jerusalem, Bethany	21:1–9	11:1–11	19:28–44	12:12–19
Monday	(2) Fig tree cursed and temple cleansed	Bethany to Jerusalem	21:10–19	11:12–18	19:45–48	

DATE	EVENT	LOCATION	MATTHEW	MARK	LUKE	JOHN
JESUS' FINAL WEEK AROUND AND IN JERUSALEM (CONT.)						
	(3) The necessity of sacrifice	Jerusalem				12:20–50
Tuesday	(4) Withered fig tree testifies	Bethany to Jerusalem	21:20–22	11:19–26		
	(5) Sanhedrin challenges Jesus. He answers by parables: two sons, workers in the vineyard and marriage feast	Jerusalem	21:23—22:14	11:27—12:12	20:1–19	
	(6) Tribute to Caesar	Jerusalem	22:15–22	12:13–17	20:20–26	
	(7) Sadducees question the resurrection	Jerusalem	22:23–33	12:18–27	20:27–40	
	(8) Pharisees question commandments	Jerusalem	22:34–40	12:28–34		
	(9) Jesus and David	Jerusalem	22:41–46	12:35–37	20:41–44	
	(10) Jesus' last sermon	Jerusalem	23:1–39	12:38–40	20:45–47	
	(11) Widow's offering	Jerusalem		12:41–44	21:1–4	
	(12) Jesus tells of the future	Mount of Olives	24:1–51	13:1–37	21:5–36	
	(13) Parables: ten virgins, talents, the day of judgment	Mount of Olives	25:1–46			
	(14) Jesus tells date of crucifixion		26:1–5	14:1–2	22:1–2	
	(15) Anointing by Mary at Simon the Leper's feast	Bethany	26:6–13	14:3–9		12:2–8
	(16) Judas contracts the betrayal		26:14–16	14:10–11	22:3–6	
Thursday	(17) Preparation for the Passover	Jerusalem	26:17–19	14:12–16	22:7–13	
Thursday p.m.	(18) Passover eaten, jealousy rebuked	Jerusalem	26:20	14:17	22:14–16, 24–30	
	(19) Feet washed	Upper Room				13:1–20
	(20) Judas revealed, defects	Upper Room	26:21–25	14:18–21	22:21–23	13:21–30
	(21) Jesus warns about further desertion; cries of loyalty	Upper Room	26:31–35	14:27–31	22:31–38	13:31–38
	(22) The last supper	Upper Room	26:26–29	14:22–25	22:17–20	
	(23) Last speech to the apostles and intercessory prayer	Jerusalem				14:1—17:26
Thursday-Friday	(24) The grief of Gethsemane	Mount of Olives	26:30, 36–46	14:26, 32–42	22:39–46	18:1
Friday	(25) Betrayal, arrest, desertion	Gethsemane	26:47–56	14:43–52	22:47–53	18:2–12
	(26) First examined by Annas	Jerusalem				18:13–14, 19–23
	(27) Trial by Caiaphas and Sanhedrin; following indignities	Jerusalem	26:57, 59–68	14:53, 55–65	22:54a, 63–65	18:24
Friday	(28) Peter's triple denial	Jerusalem	26:58, 69–75	14:54, 66–72	22:54b–62	18:15–18, 25–27
	(29) Condemnation by the Sanhedrin	Jerusalem	27:1	15:1a	22:66–71	
	(30) Suicide of Judas	Jerusalem	27:3–10			
	(31) First appearance before Pilate	Jerusalem	27:2,11–14	15:1b–5	23:1–6	18:28–38

DATE	EVENT	LOCATION	MATTHEW	MARK	LUKE	JOHN
JESUS' FINAL WEEK AROUND AND IN JERUSALEM (CONT.)						
	(32) Jesus before Herod	Jerusalem			23:7–12	
	(33) Second appearance before Pilate	Jerusalem	27:15–26	15:6–15	23:13–25	18:39—19:16a
	(34) Mockery by Roman soldiers	Jerusalem	27:27–30	15:16–19		
	(35) Led to Golgotha	Jerusalem	27:31–34	15:20–23	23:26–32	19:16b–17
	(36) Events of first three hours on cross	Golgotha	27:35–44	15:24–32	23:33–43	19:18–27
Friday	(37) Last three hours on cross	Golgotha	27:45–50	15:33–37	23:44,46	19:28–30
	(38) Events attending Jesus' death		27:51–56	15:38–41	23:45, 47–49	
	(39) Burial of Jesus	Jerusalem	27:57–61	15:42–46	23:50–54	19:31–42
Friday-Saturday	(40) Tomb sealed	Jerusalem	27:62–66			
	(41) Women watch	Jerusalem		15:47	23:55–56	
THE RESURRECTION THROUGH THE ASCENSION						
AD 30						
Dawn of First Day (Sunday, "Lord's Day")	(1) Women visit the tomb	Near Jerusalem	28:1–8	16:1–8	24:1–11	20:1–2
	(2) Peter and John see the empty tomb				24:12	20:3–10
	(3) Jesus' appearance to Mary Magdalene	Jerusalem		[16:9–11]		20:11–18
	(4) Jesus' appearance to the other women	Jerusalem	28:9–10			
	(5) Guards' report of the resurrection		28:11–15			
Sunday Afternoon	(6) Jesus' appearance to two disciples on way to Emmaus			[16:12–13]	24:13–35	
Late Sunday	(7) Jesus' appearance to ten disciples without Thomas	Jerusalem			24:36–43	20:19–25
One Week Later	(8) Appearance to disciples with Thomas	Jerusalem			24:44–49	20:26–31
During 40 Days until Ascension	(9) Jesus' appearance to seven disciples by Sea of Galilee	Galilee				21:1–25
	(10) Great Commission		28:16–20	[16:14–18]		
	(11) The Ascension	Mount Olivet		[16:19–20]	24:50–53	

Join Alli at her

Upcoming Events

Woman Camp

womancamp.us

Ignite Conference

crossroads.net/ignite

Let Alli Help You
Build What Lasts

★★★★★

Blueprint for Belonging

Build your relationships like Jesus did.

★★★★★

How to Stay Standing

Build your life on a solid foundation.

Discover **NEW STUDIES** from teachers you love, and **NEW TEACHERS** we know you'll love!

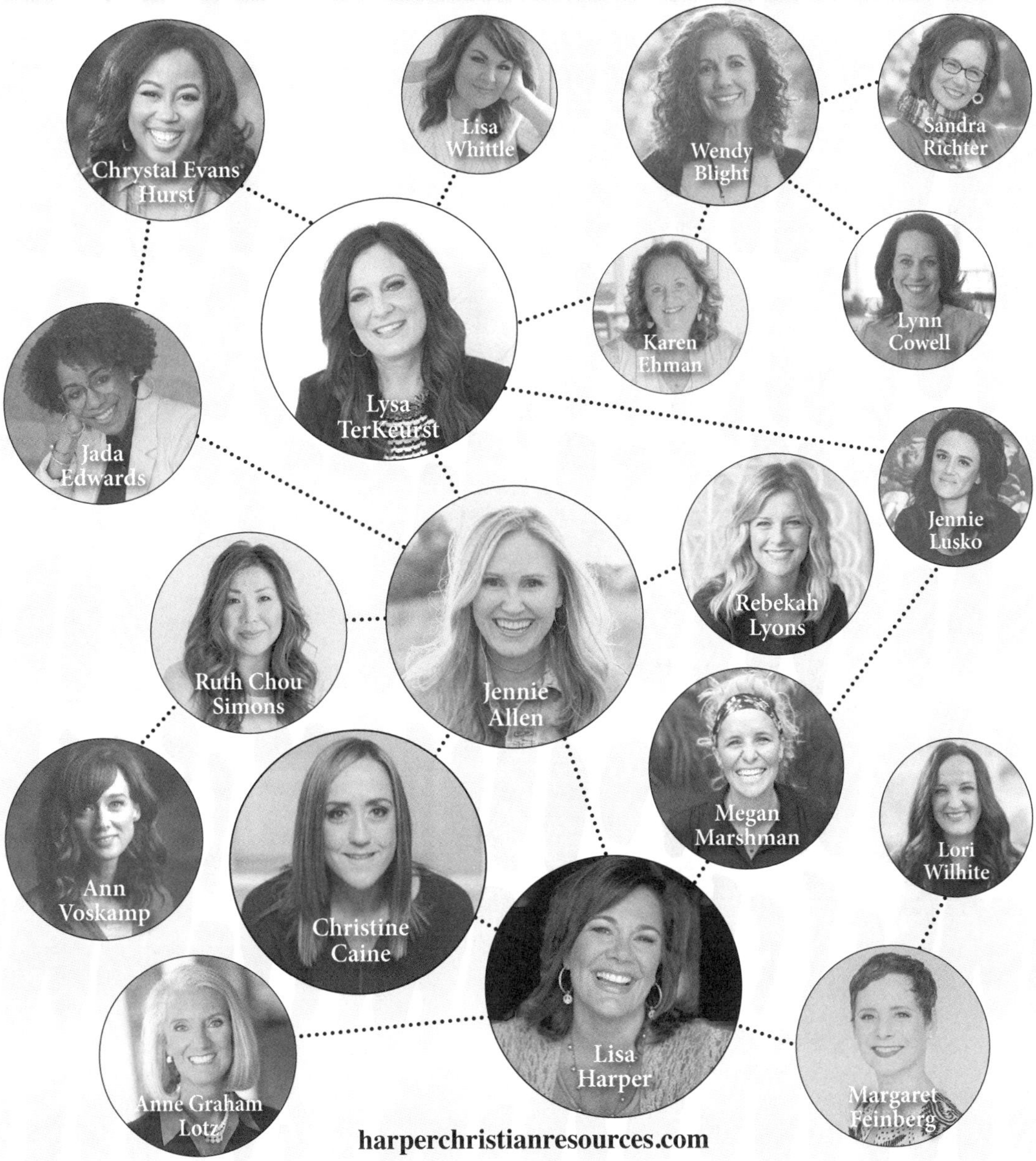

Chrystal Evans Hurst

Lisa Whittle

Wendy Blight

Sandra Richter

Lysa TerKeurst

Karen Ehman

Lynn Cowell

Jada Edwards

Jennie Lusko

Rebekah Lyons

Ruth Chou Simons

Jennie Allen

Megan Marshman

Ann Voskamp

Christine Caine

Lori Wilhite

Lisa Harper

Anne Graham Lotz

Margaret Feinberg

harperchristianresources.com

From the Publisher

GREAT STUDIES

ARE EVEN BETTER WHEN THEY'RE SHARED!

Help others find this study:

- Post a review at your favorite online bookseller.
- Post a picture on a social media account and share why you enjoyed it.
- Send a note to a friend who would also love it—or, better yet, go through it with them!

Thanks for helping others grow their faith!